BRAIN GAM

Get Ready for
SCIENCE

Picture Puzzles
for Growing Minds

pil

Publications International, Ltd.

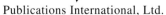

Images from Shutterstock.com

Brain Games is a registered trademark of Publications International, Ltd.

Louis Weber, CEO
Publications International, Ltd.
8140 Lehigh Avenue
Morton Grove, IL 60053

ISBN: 978-1-64558-844-3

Manufactured in China.

8 7 6 5 4 3 2 1

What is STEM?

The acronym STEM stands for Science, Technology, Engineering, and Math. STEM is not just about knowledge, but also about how to obtain, process, and apply that knowledge. The skills involved include observation, investigation, understanding, and problem-solving. Introducing these concepts early on can help foster children's curiosity and build the skills they need to understand the world around them.

Play to LEARN.

The picture puzzles in this book encourage children to explore and learn, even as they play! Sometimes puzzlers are encouraged to look closely at a picture for details, or to take a wider view to plan their path through a maze. At other times, they can try out their logic skills to solve the puzzle. Throughout the book, bright, colorful pictures and challenging games keep children interested and entertained.

The puzzles may be done in any order, and with or without help from an adult. Kids can check the table of contents to find their favorite types of puzzles, or dive straight in!

Contents

Critical Thinking

Experiment

Observation

Contents

Problem-solving

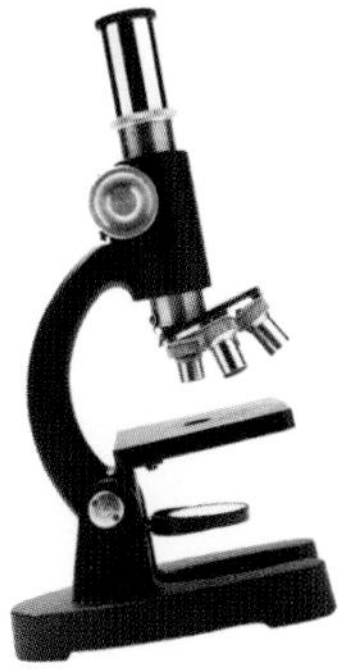

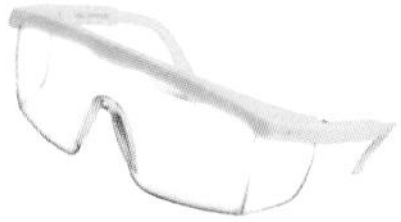

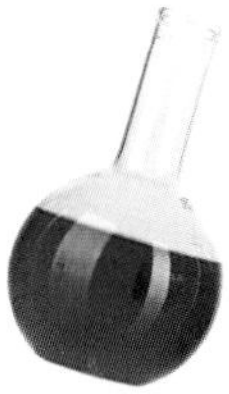

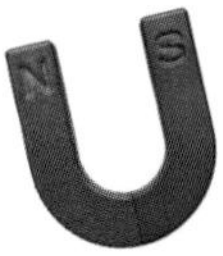
N
S

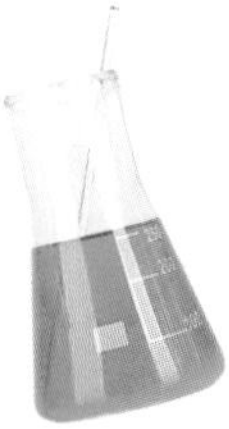

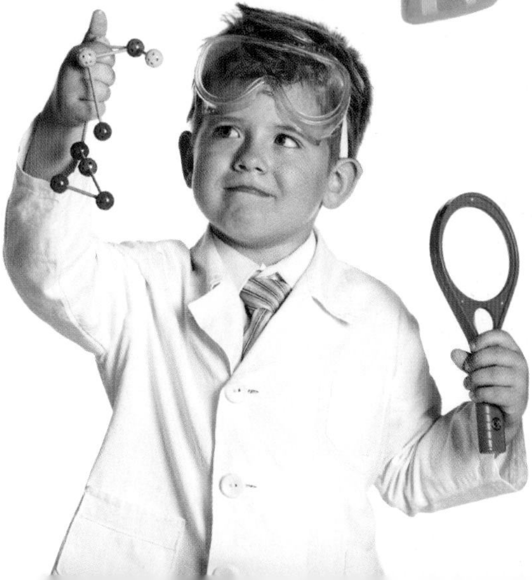

Match It

Draw a line from each animal to one of the same kind. A mammal goes with a mammal, a bird to a bird, insect to insect, and so on.

Answers on page 107.

What's Next?

These turtles are doing something in each photo. What will they do next?

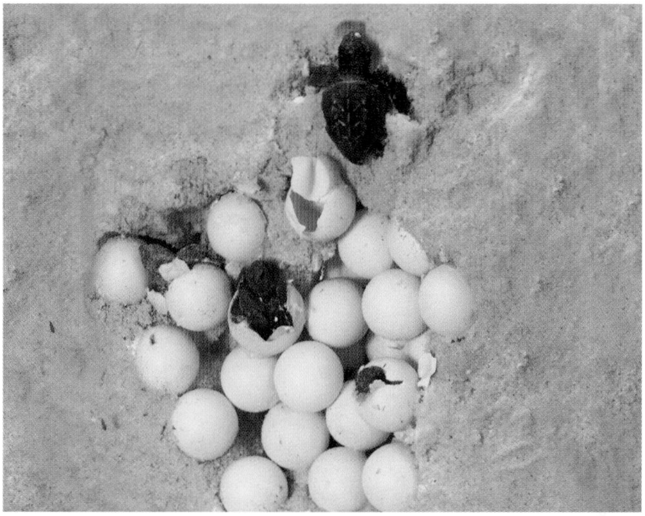

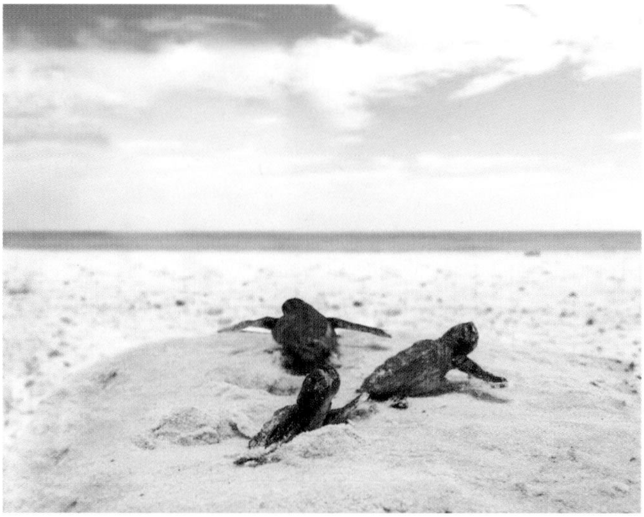

Answers on page 107.

What Do I Do?

What am I? What do I help people do?

Answers on page 107.

Something's Wrong

What is wrong in this picture? Find 3 mistakes.

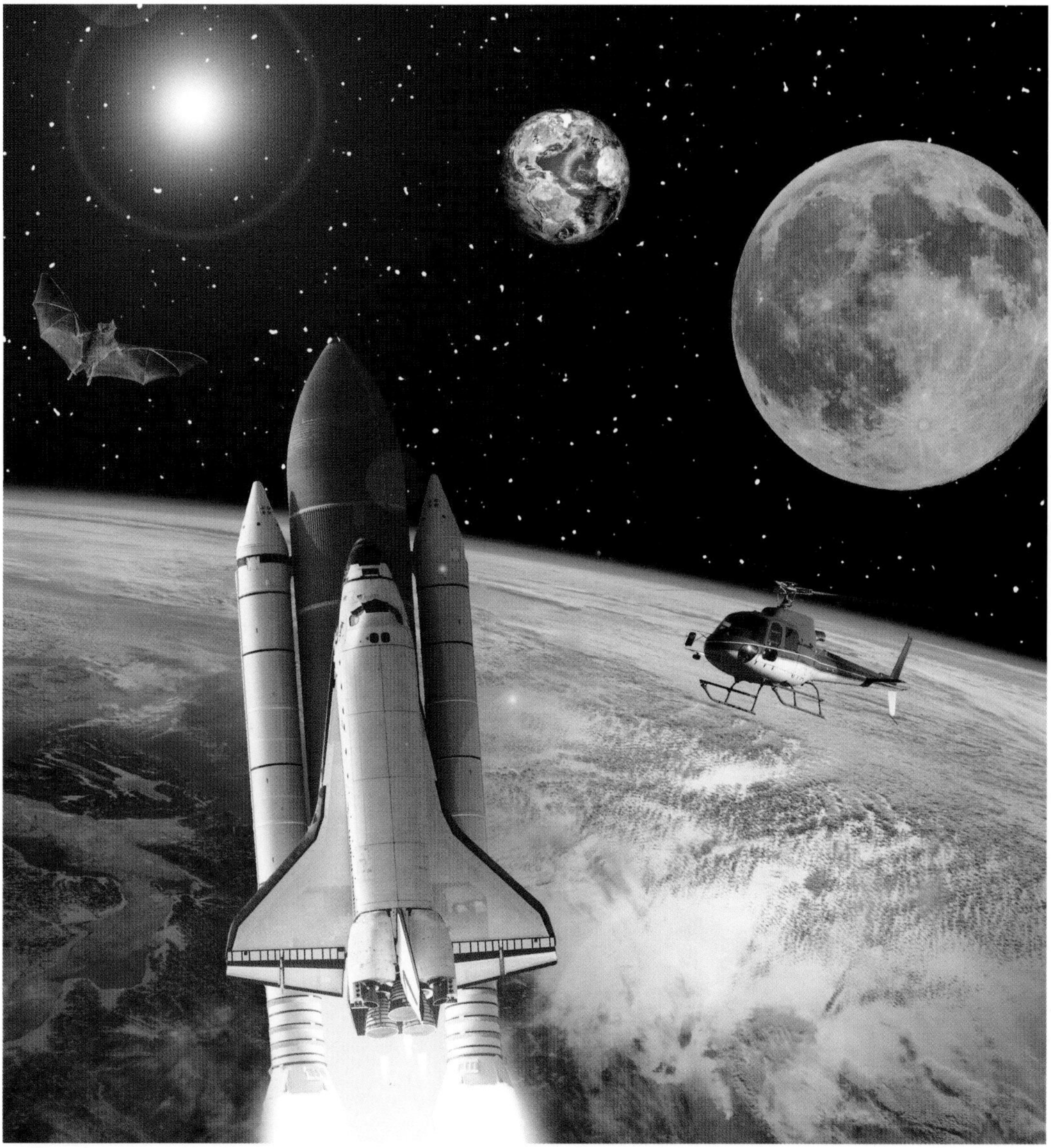

Answers on page 107.

Where Am I?

Point to the parts of the plant:

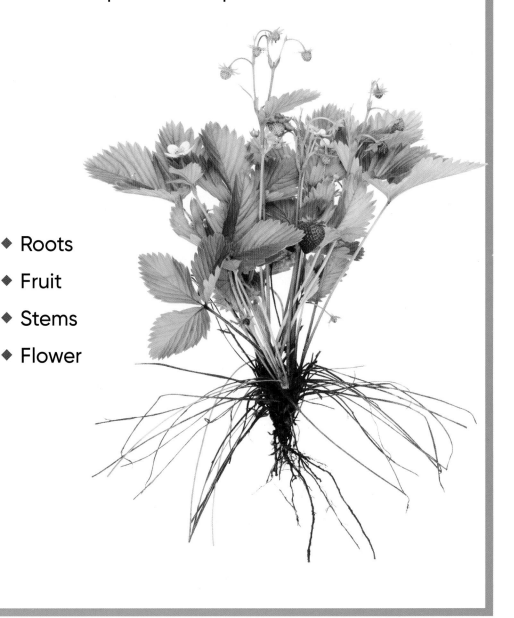

◆ Roots

◆ Fruit

◆ Stems

◆ Flower

Answers on page 108.

Do It

Hit the page! What do you think will happen?
Turn the page to find out.

What happened?

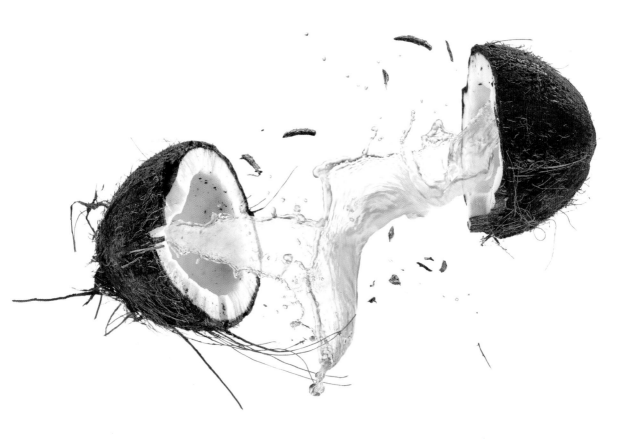

Answers on page 108.

On the Right Path

Follow the path that goes through every planet. But avoid the black hole!

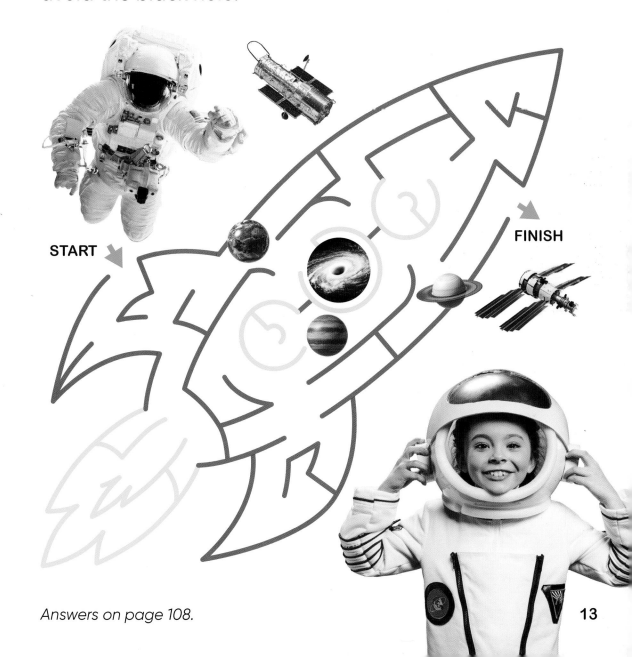

START

FINISH

Answers on page 108.

13

What's Different?

Circle the 5 differences between these pictures.

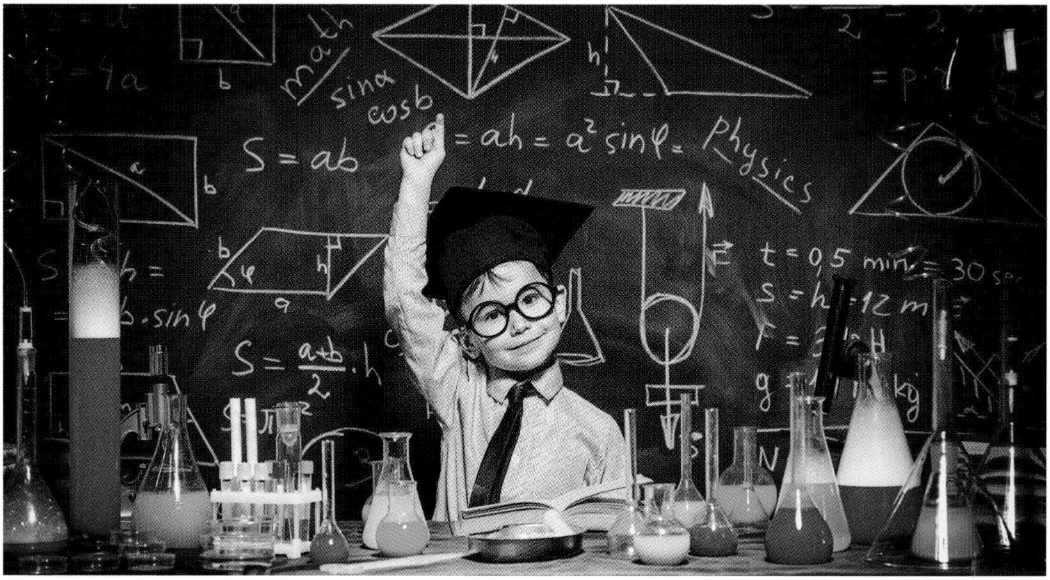
math
S = ab
Physics

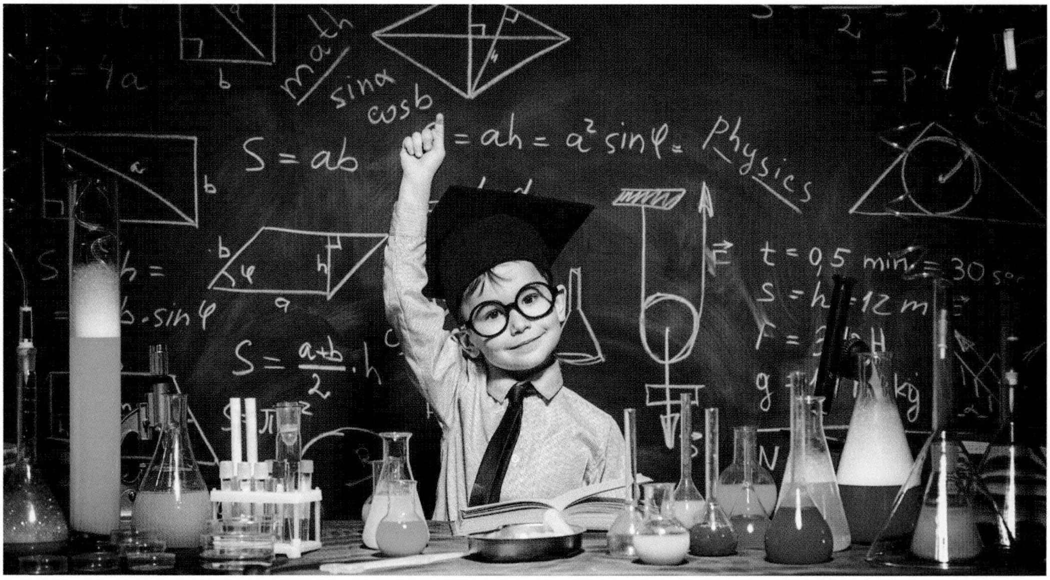
math
S = ab
Physics

Answers on page 108.

Patterns

Finish each pattern.

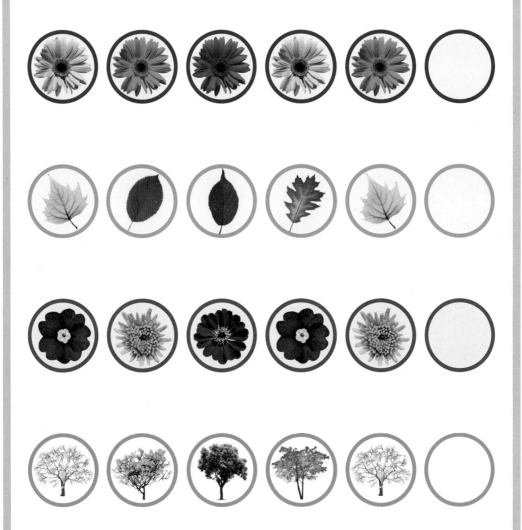

On the Right Path

Find the path that goes through every fossil. But avoid the dinosaurs!

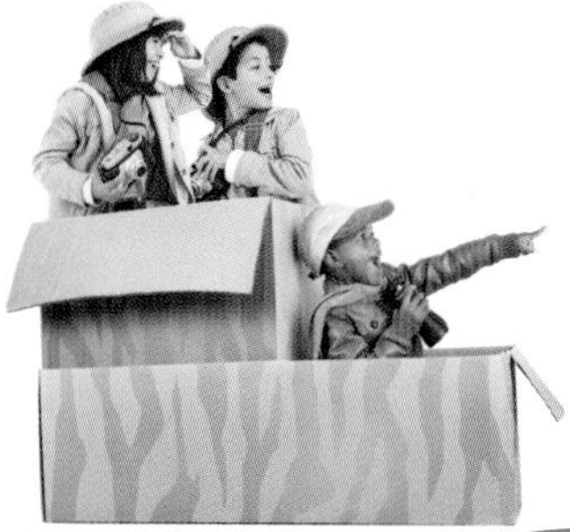

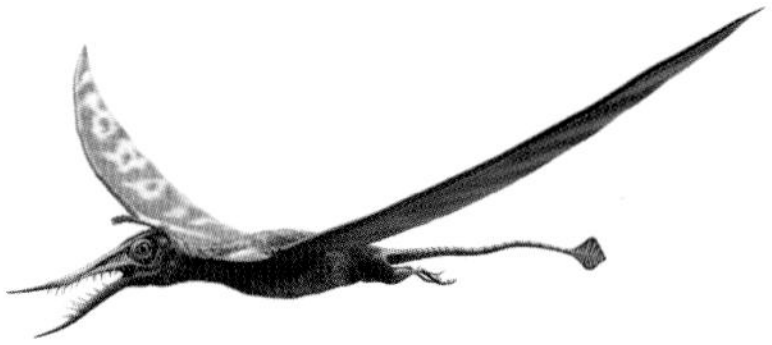

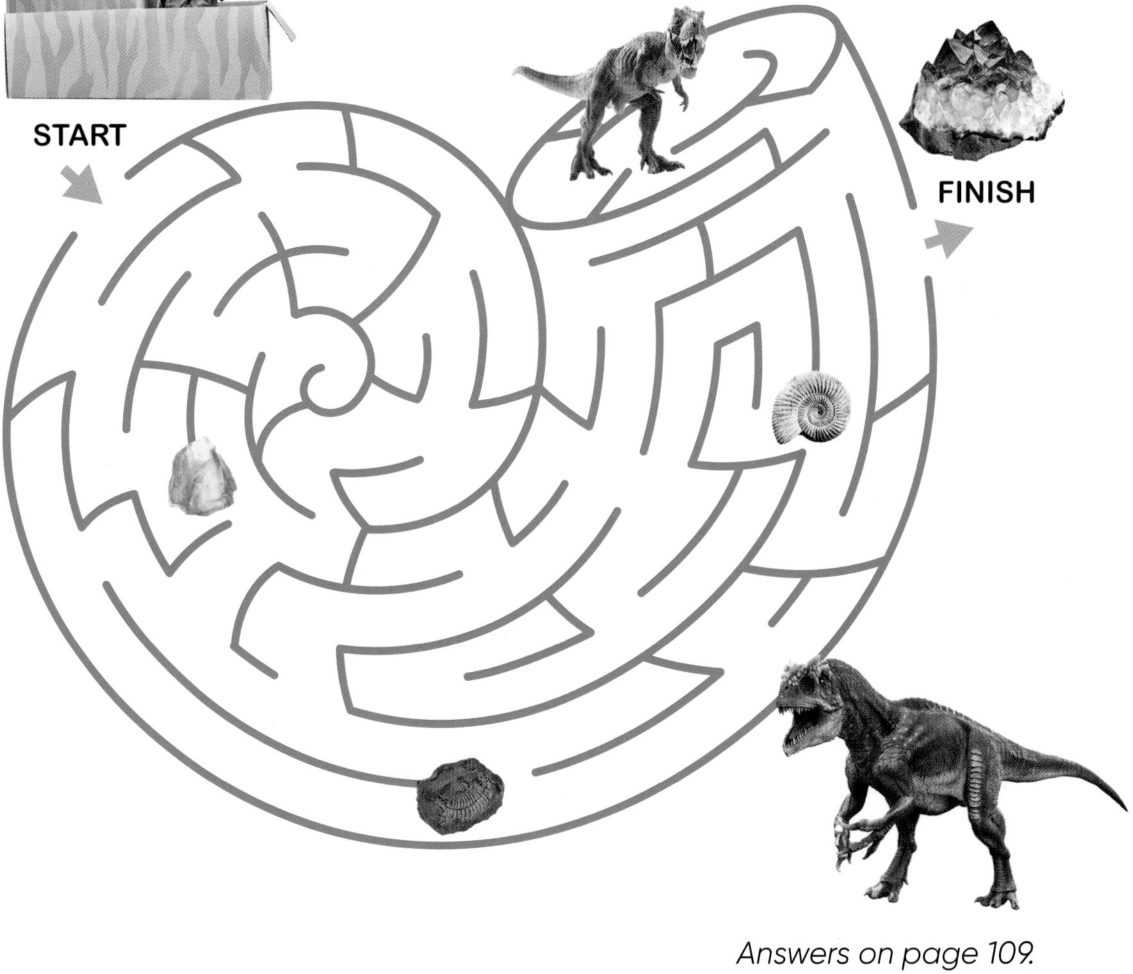
START
FINISH

Answers on page 109.

Memory

Look at this picture for 1 minute. Remember as much as you can! Then turn the page.

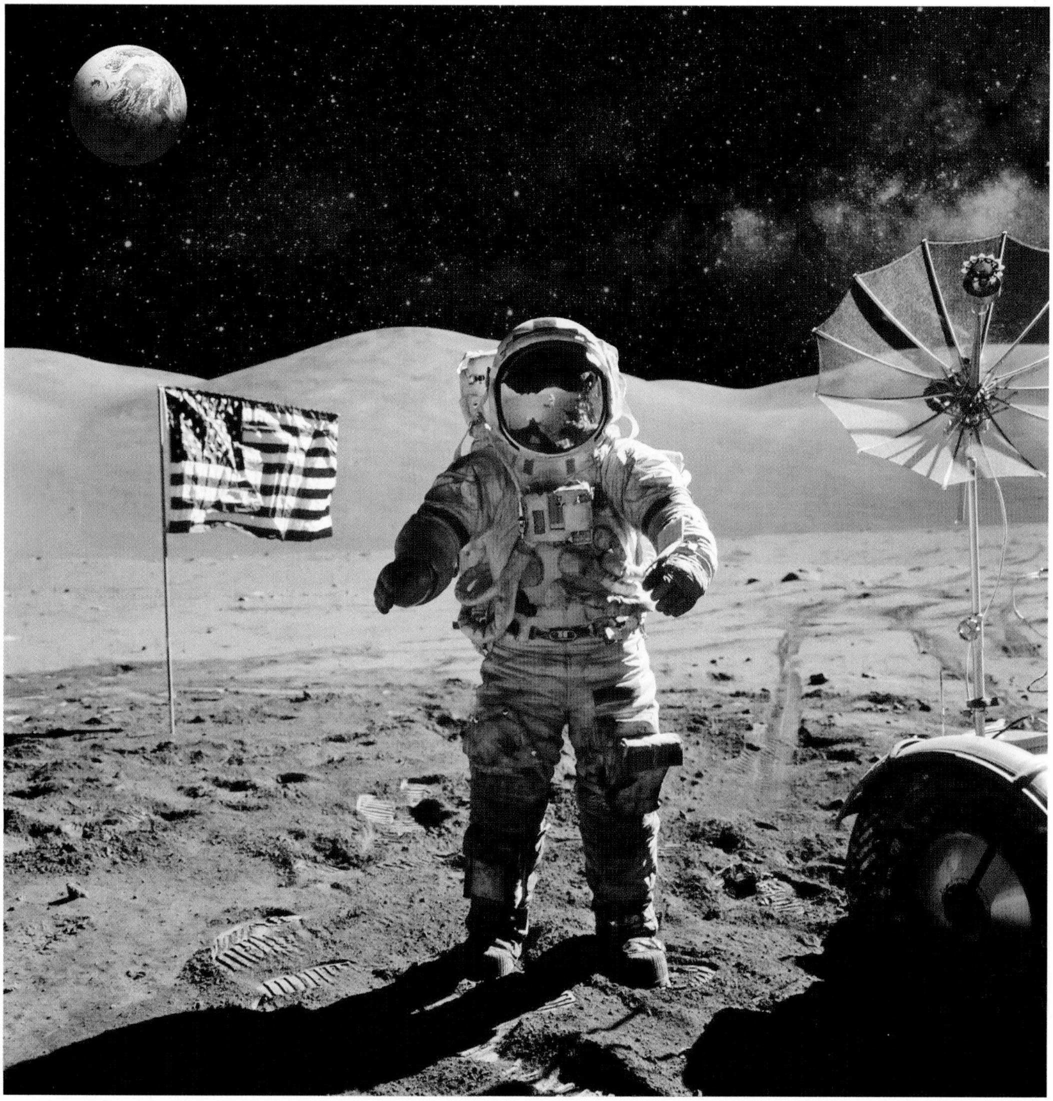

What is different in this picture? Find 3 things that are different.

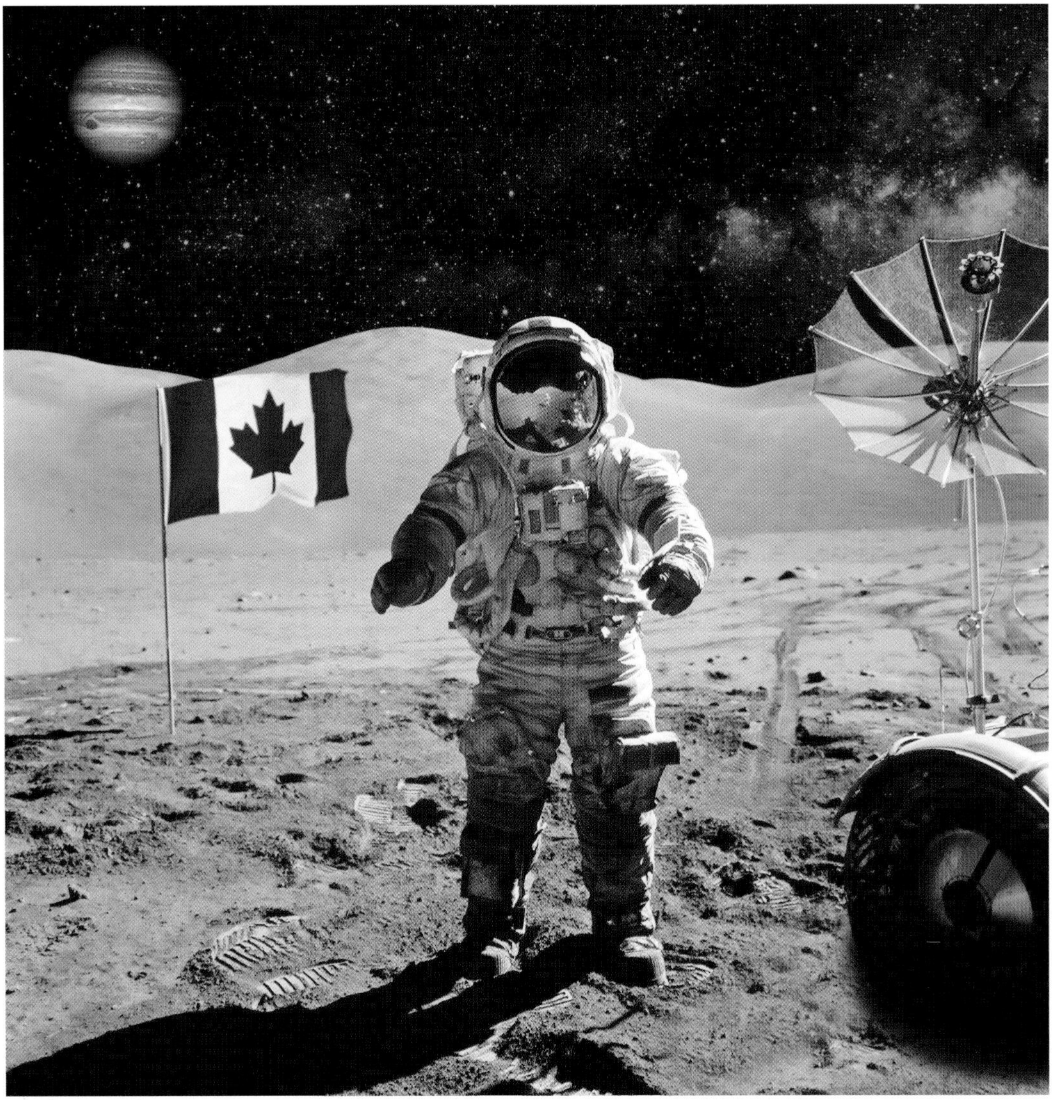

Answers on page 109.

What Do I Do?

What am I? What do people use me for?

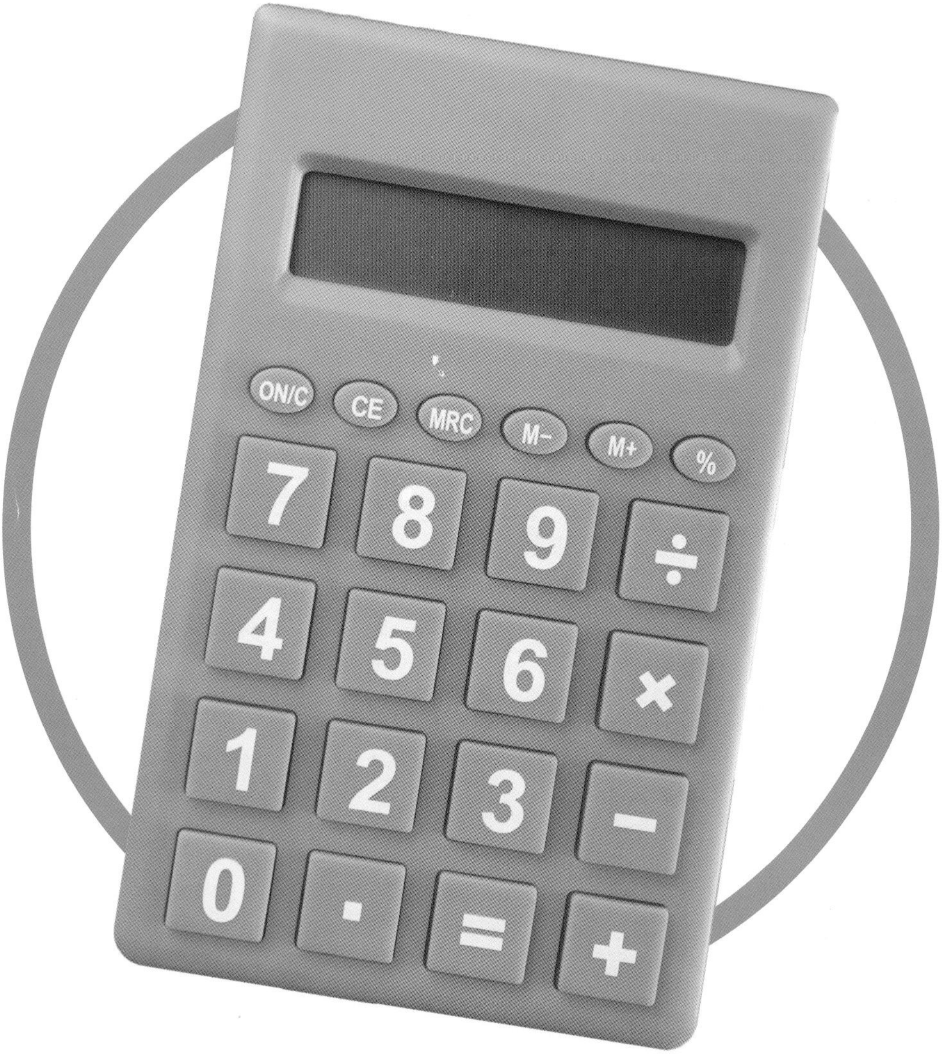
ON/C
CE
MRC
M-
M+
%
7
8
9
÷
4
5
6
×
1
2
3
–
0
.
=
+

Answers on page 109.

Corner of Your Eye

You can see things around you without moving your head or your eyes! This is called peripheral vision. You can test the limits of this vision. It takes two people to do this activity, so grab a friend.

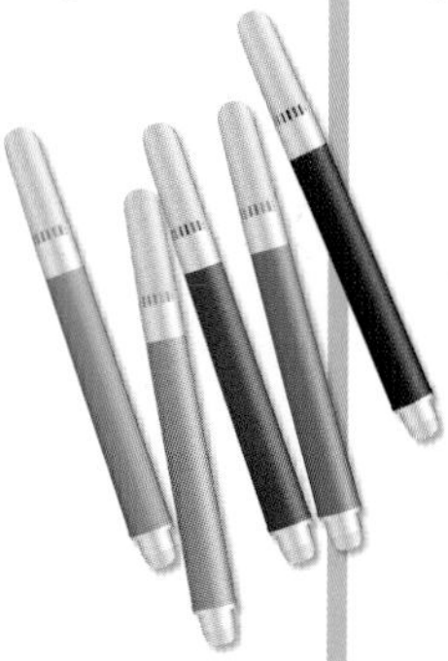
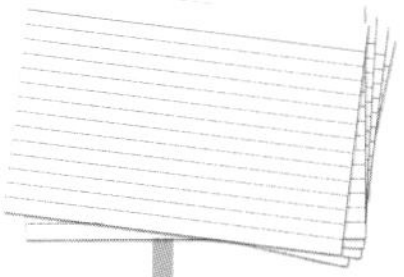

What you need:

- 1 black marker
- 4 other markers of different colors
- 5 index cards
- 6 popsicle sticks (pencils also work)
- Masking or painter's tape
- A table or desk
- A chair

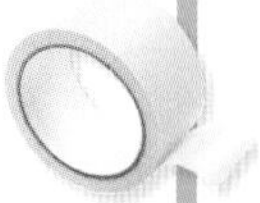
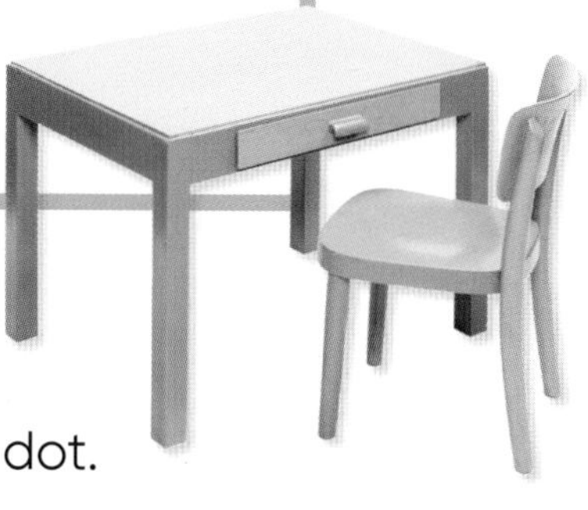

Setting up:

1. On one index card, draw a small black dot.
2. Draw on each of the other cards a different shape in a different color.
3. Tape one card to each popsicle stick.

Experiment:

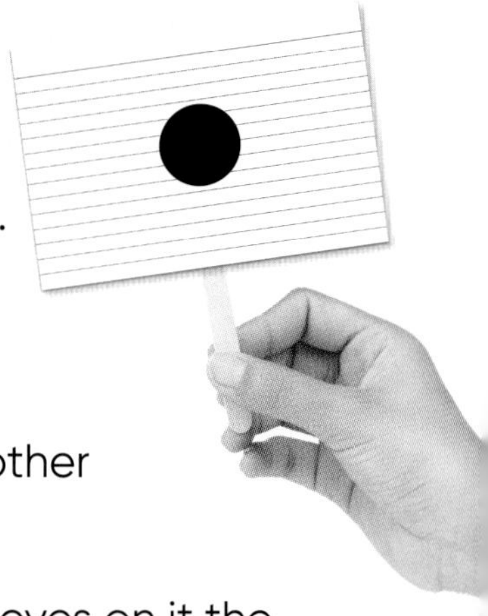

1. Sit at the table or desk. Hold the card with the black dot in one hand straight out in front of you.
2. Ask your friend to mix up the shape cards where you can't see.
3. Your friend puts one of the shape cards in your other hand without you looking at it.
4. Stare at the black dot in front of you. Keep your eyes on it the whole time. Do not move your head.
5. Hold the shape card straight out beside you. Slowly move it in an arc toward the black dot card. Remember: Don't look at it!
6. When you can see movement in the corner of your eye, stop your arm. Your friend puts a piece of tape on the table to mark that spot. Then continue slowly moving.
7. Stop so your friend can add a mark when you can tell what color the card is. Do the same for when you know what shape it is.
8. Do the same thing with the remaining three cards.

What do you see first? Last?
How far does your peripheral vision go?

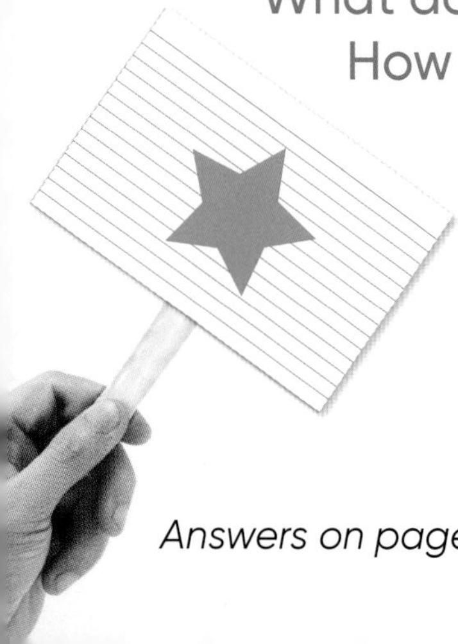

Extra challenge!

Switch hands. The moving hand now holds the black dot. Your other hand moves with a shape card.

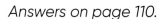

Answers on page 110.

Hide and Seek

Find these animals hiding in the forest.

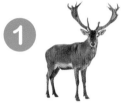

1 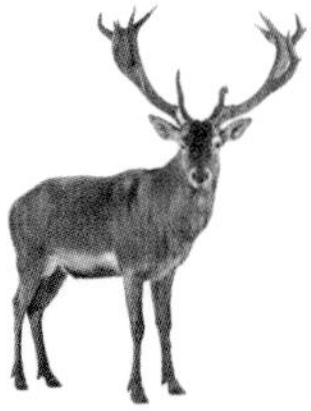

2 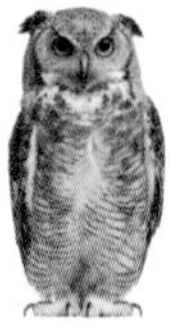

3 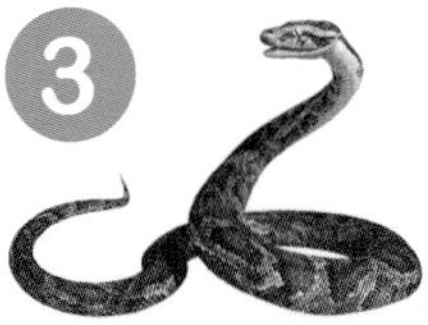

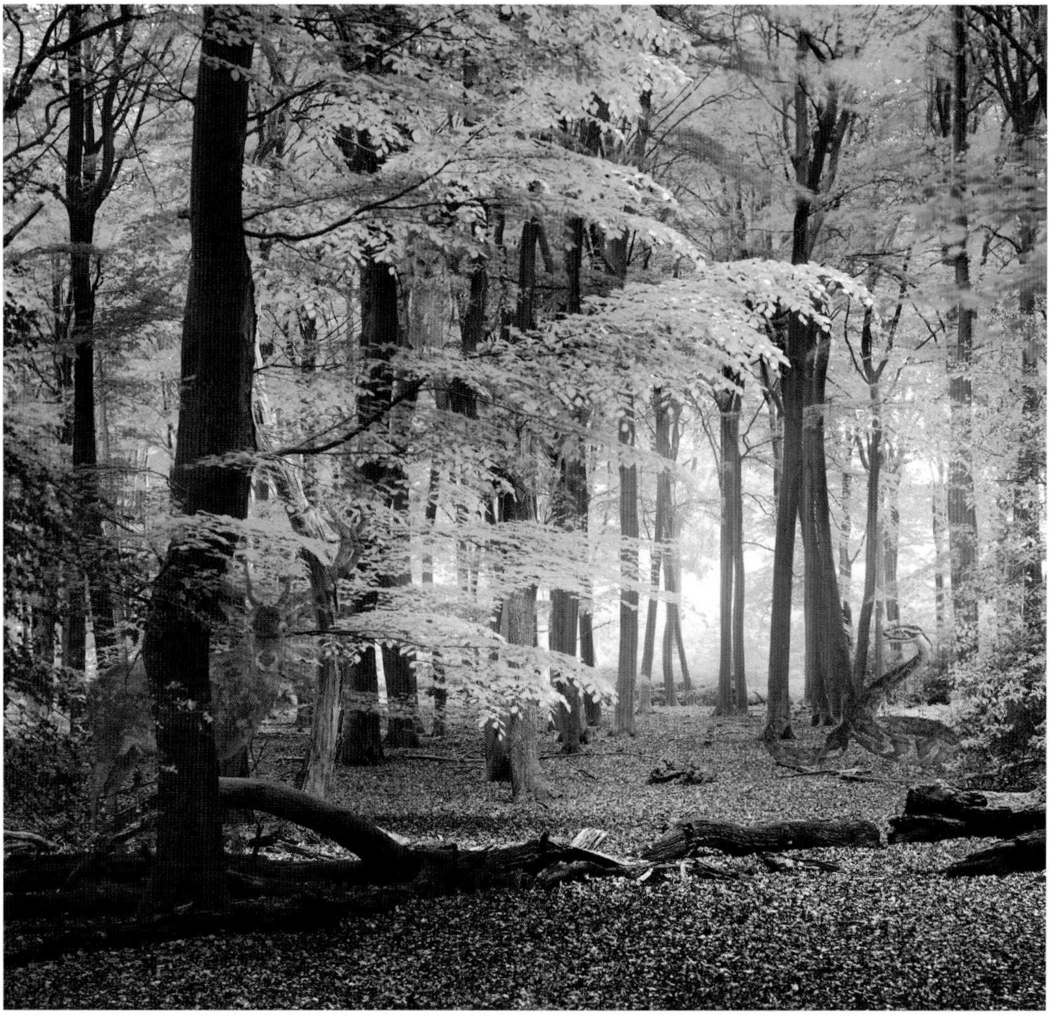

Answers on page 110.

Out of Order

These pictures are in the wrong order! What is the right order?

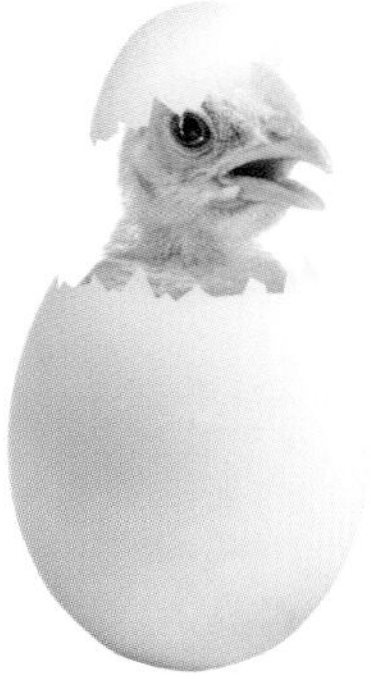

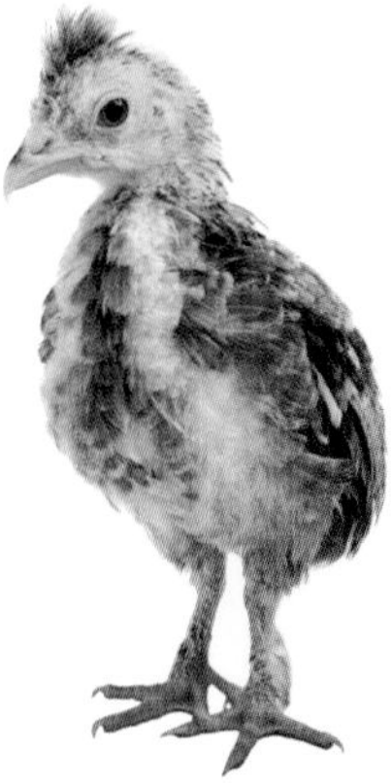

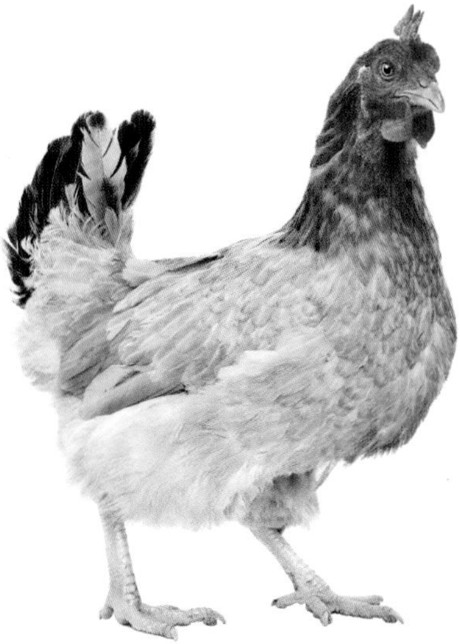

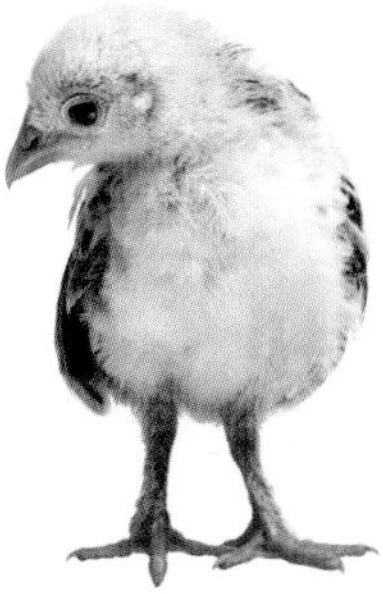

1

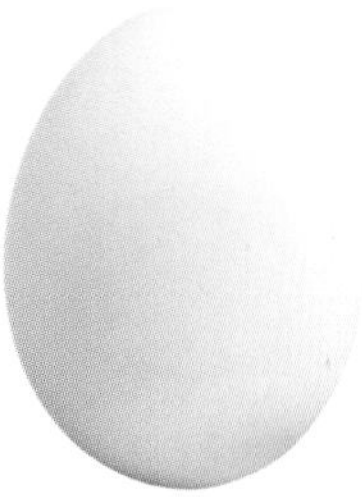

Answers on page 110.

Something's Wrong

What is wrong in this photo? Find 3 mistakes.

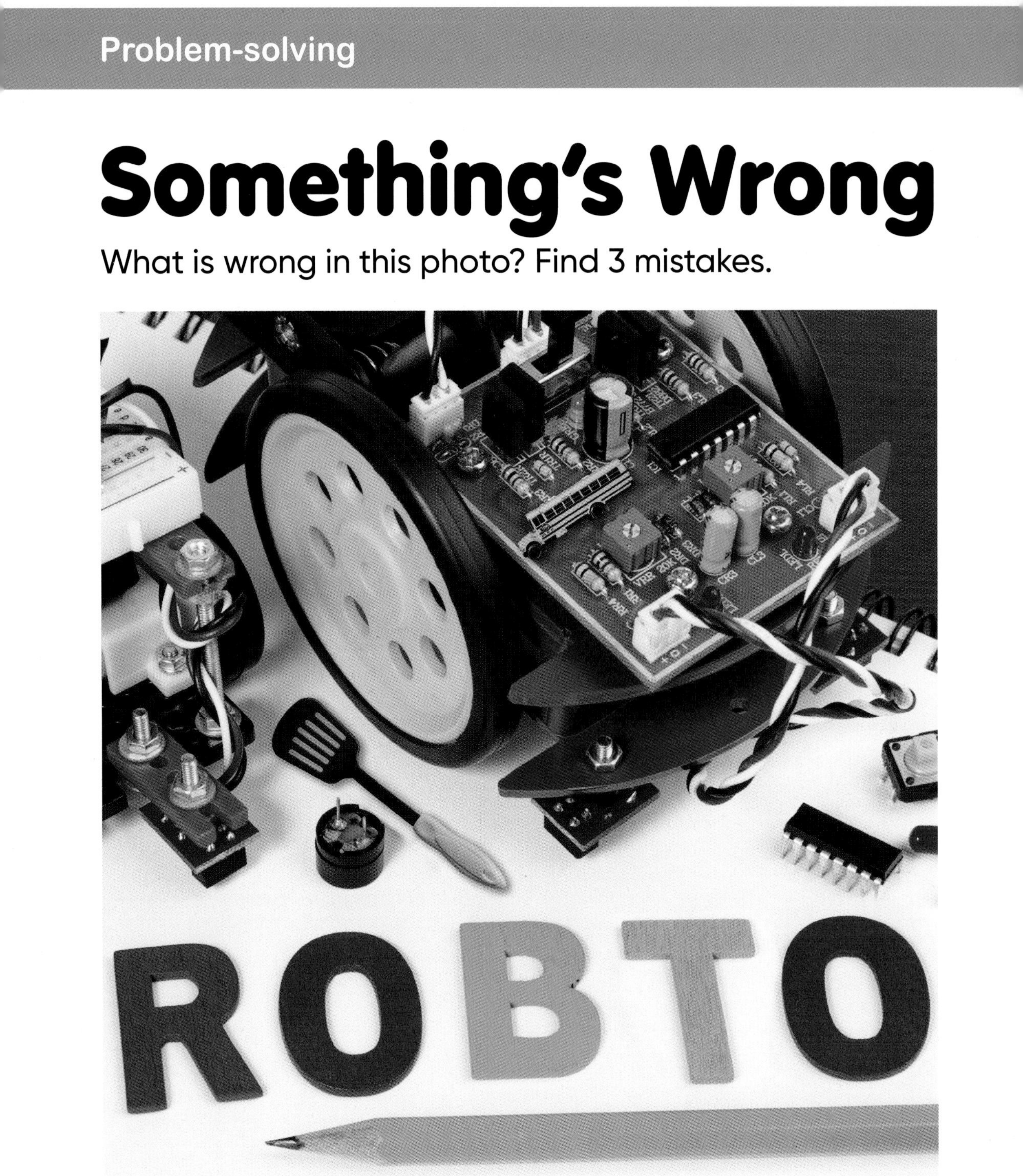
ROBTO

Answers on page 110.

Shadows

Circle the shadow that matches the binoculars.

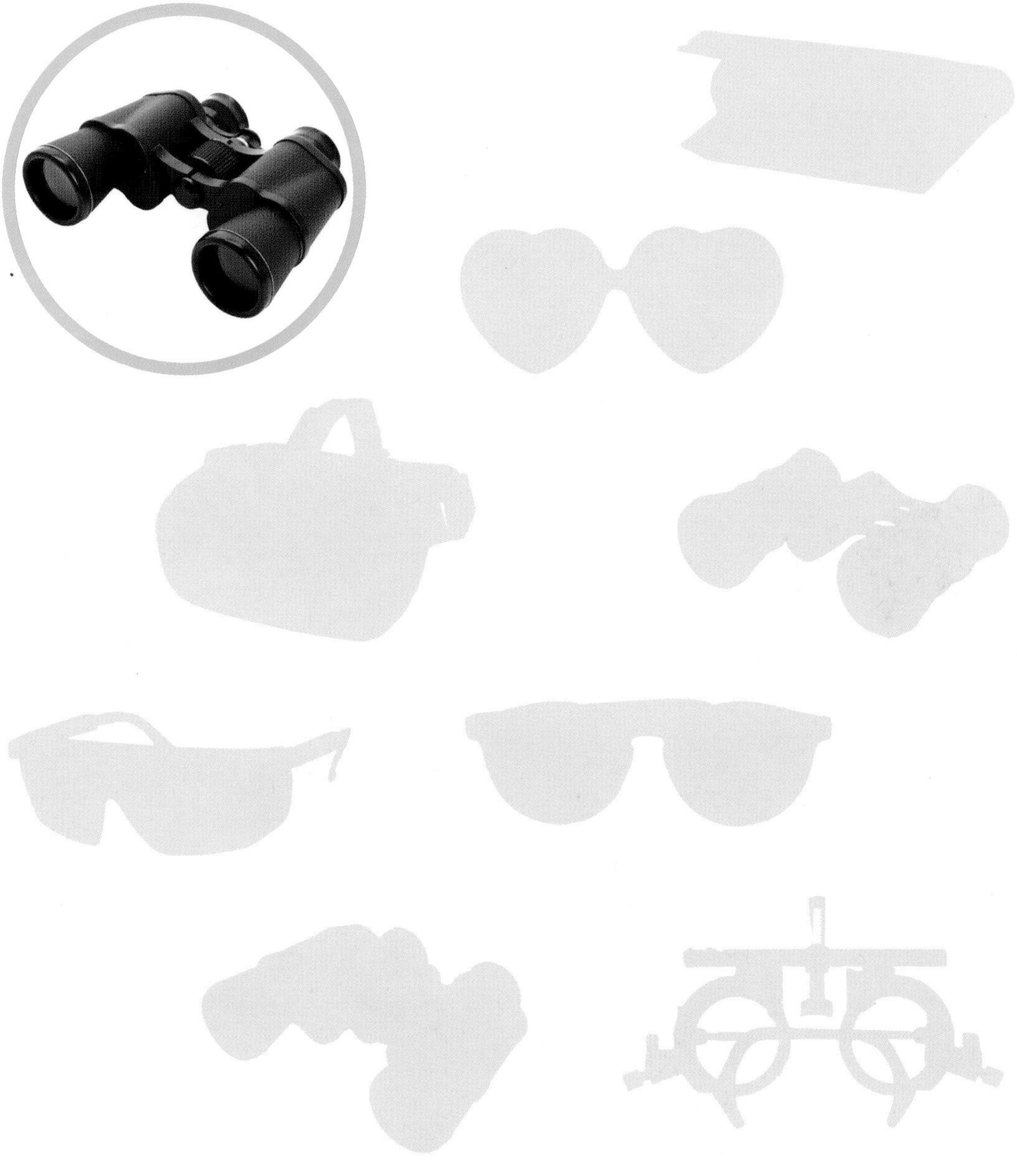

Answers on page 111.

Missing Piece

Circle the piece that goes in the missing spot.

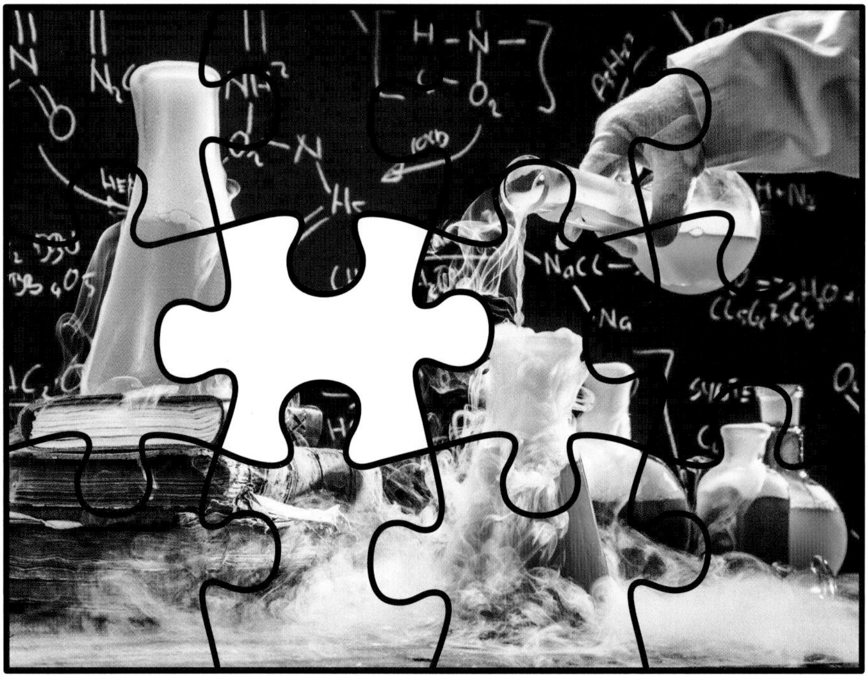

1

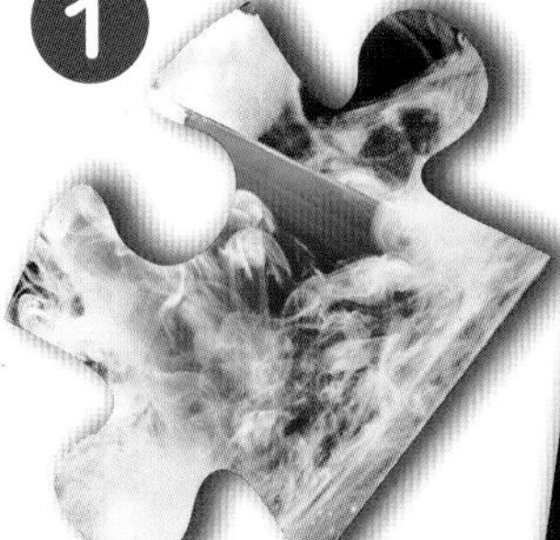

2

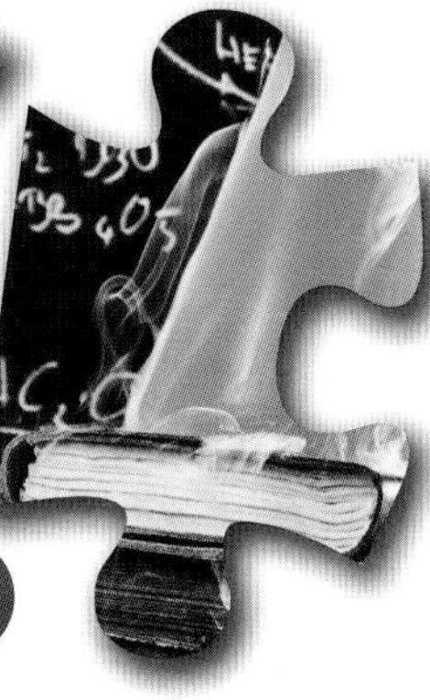

3

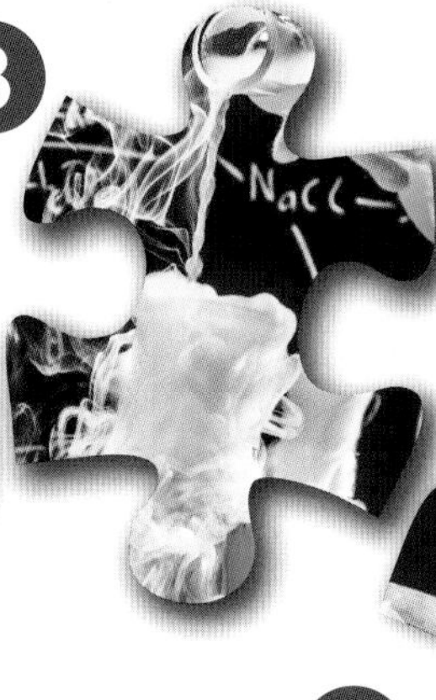

4

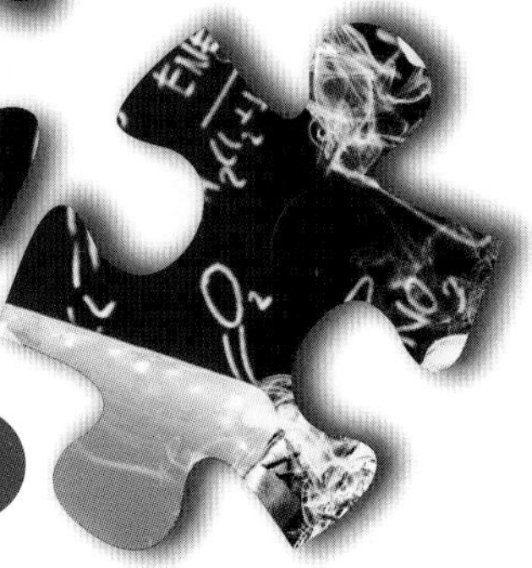

Answers on page 111.

Draw It

The hot air balloon is missing a part! Can you draw in the missing balloon?

Answers on page 111.

On the Right Path

Follow the path that goes through every seashell. But avoid the crabs!

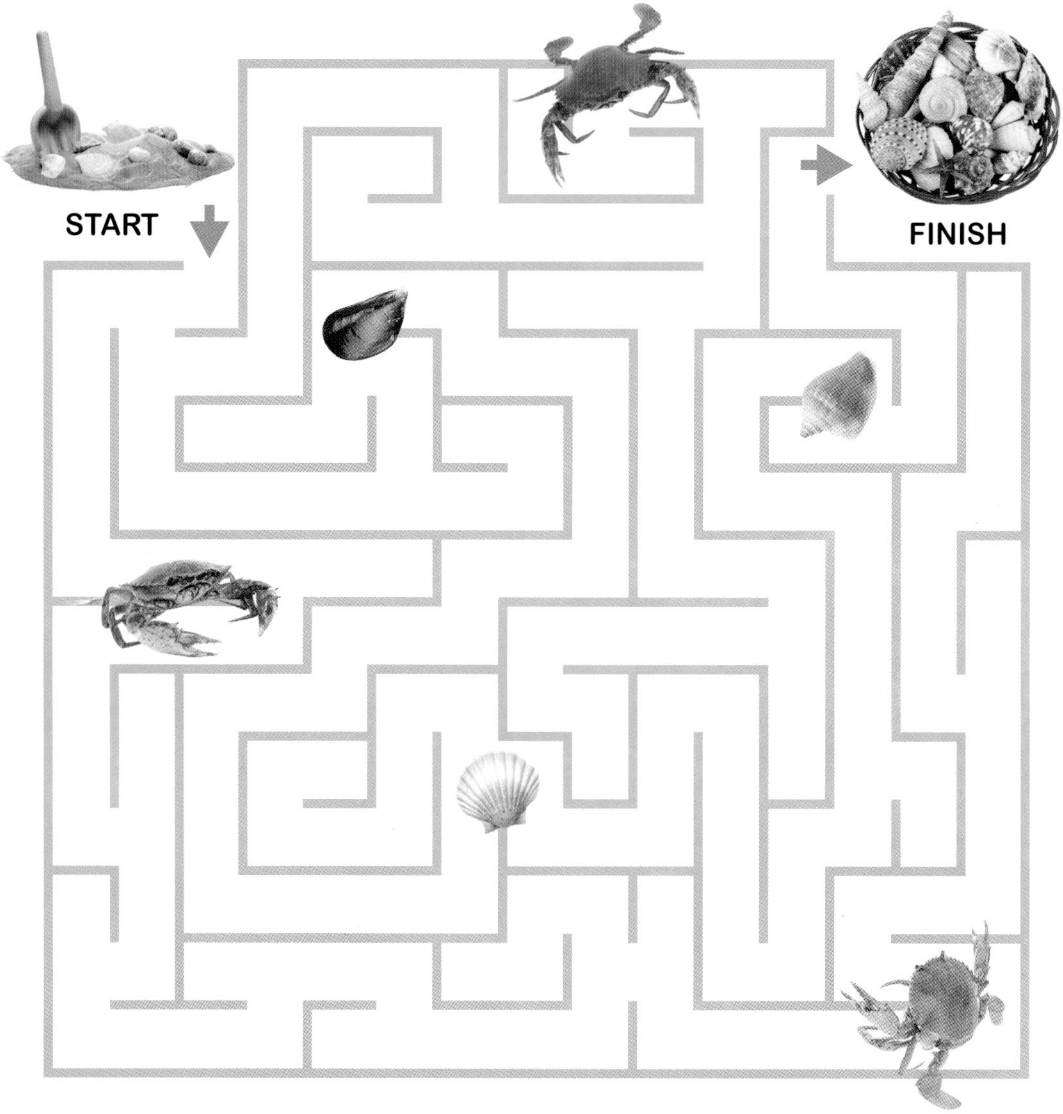
START
FINISH

Answers on page 111.

Match It

Draw a line to connect each tool to the first letter of its name.

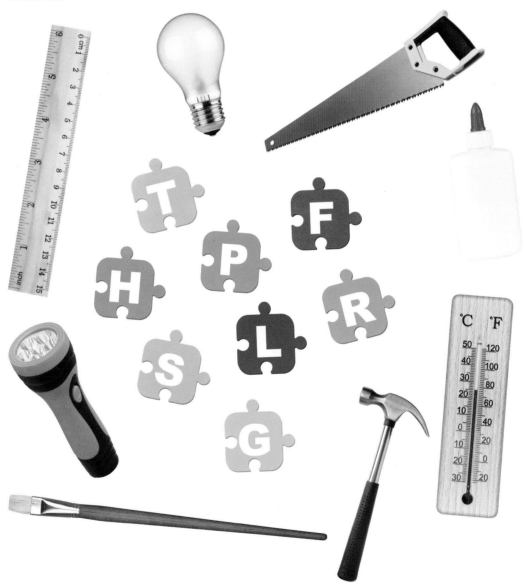

Answers on page 112.

What Is It?

These objects are all cut up! Can you see what each one is?

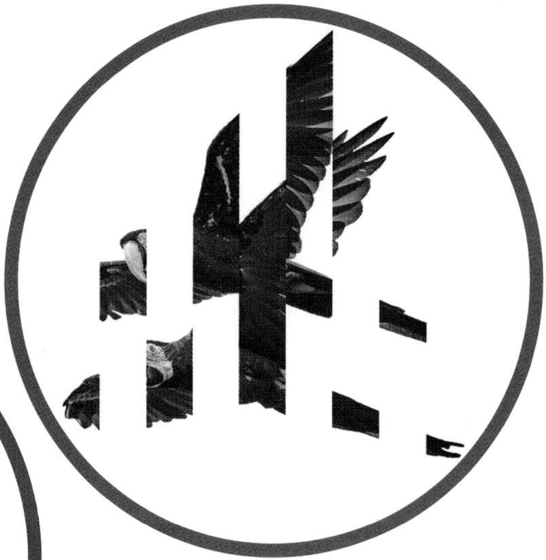

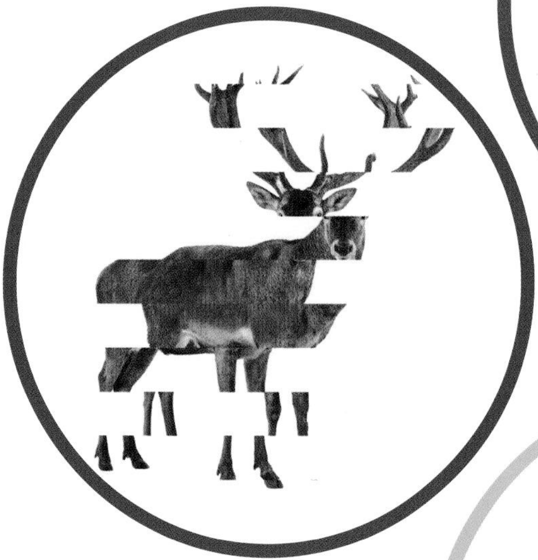

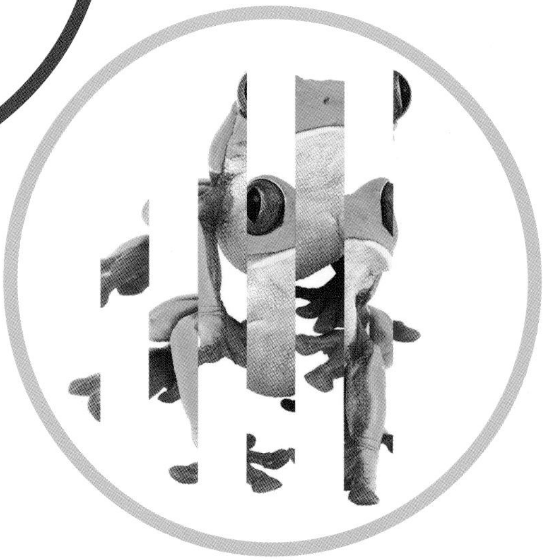

Answers on page 112.

Zoom In

Draw a line from each zoomed picture to the object it matches.

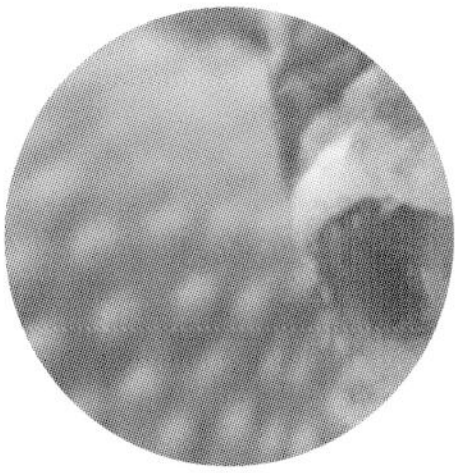
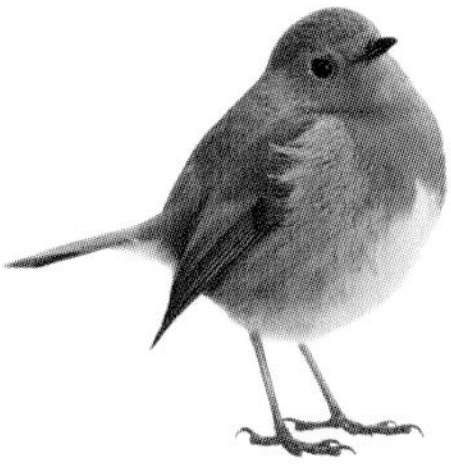
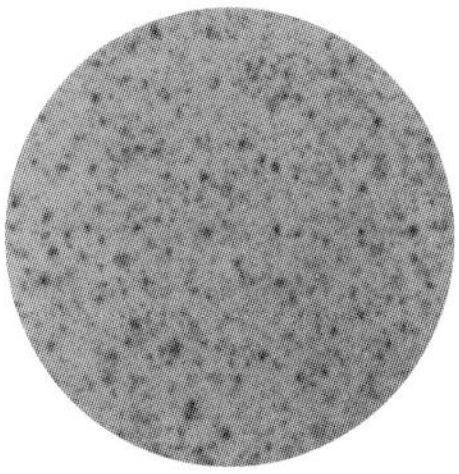
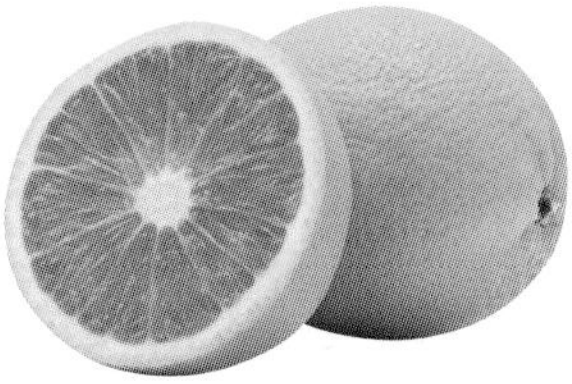
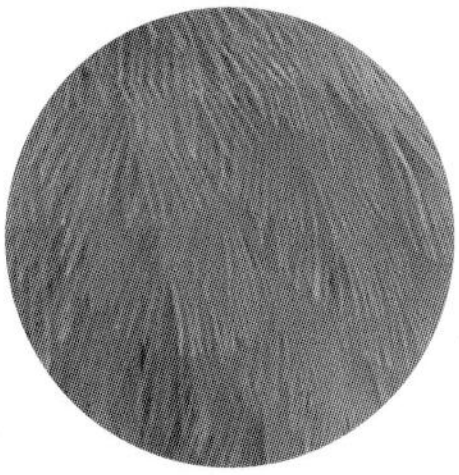
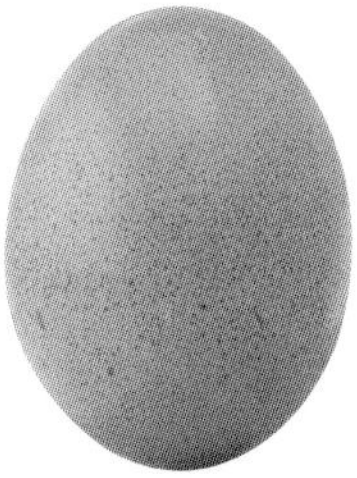
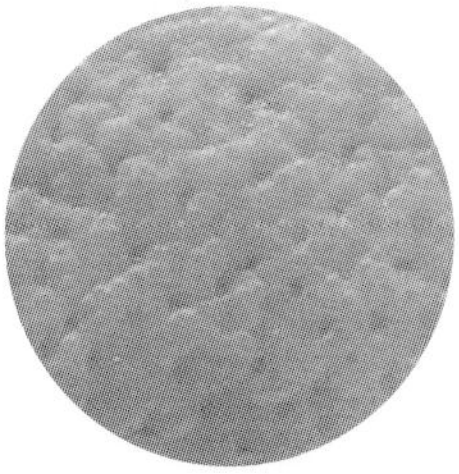
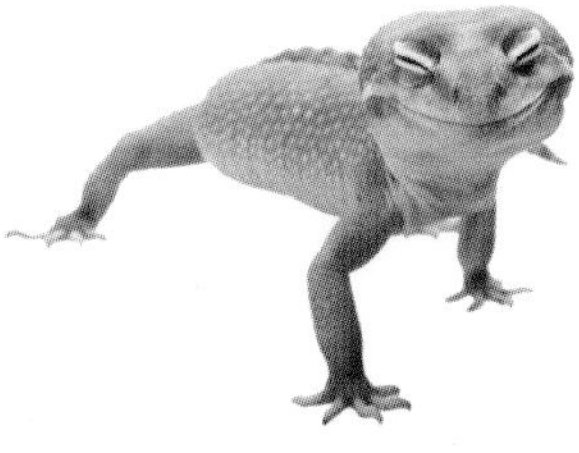

Answers on page 112.

Where Am I?

- ◆ Hands
- ◆ Ears
- ◆ Shoulders
- ◆ Feet

Answers on page 112.

Which Ones?

Circle all the animals on this page that can fly.

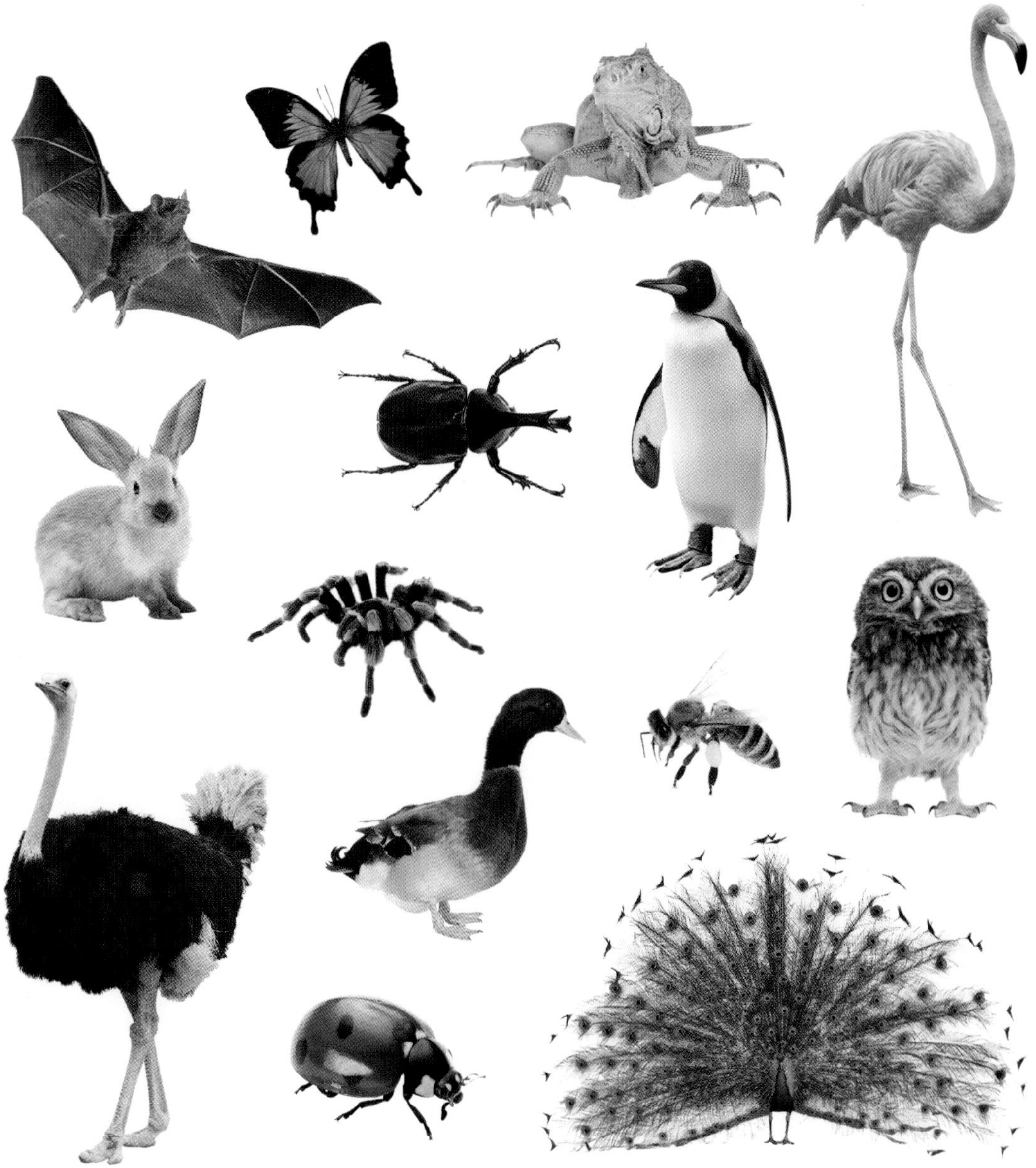

Answers on page 113.

Groups

Write the number of plants and fruits that fit in each group. Some might fit in more than one group!

Are yellow? ________

Are flowers? ________

Can be eaten? ________

Can grow in the garden? ________

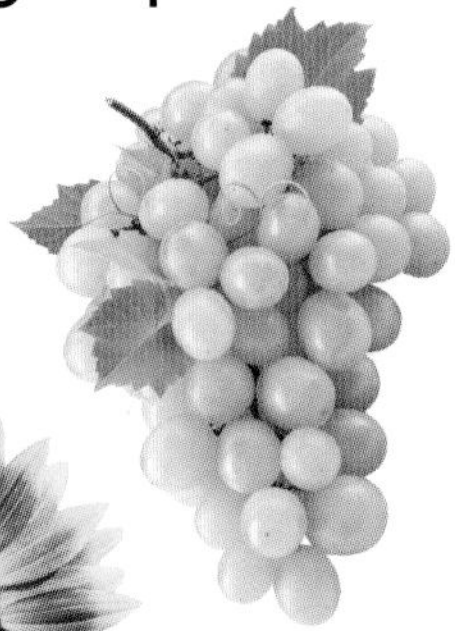
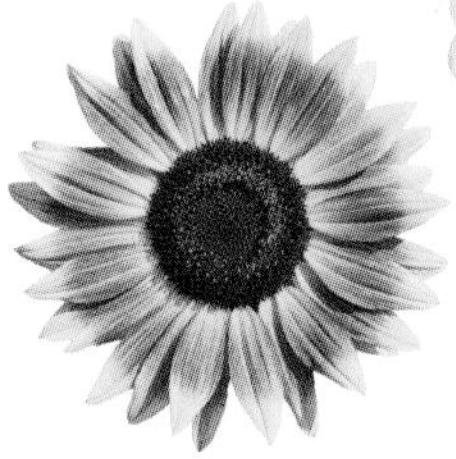
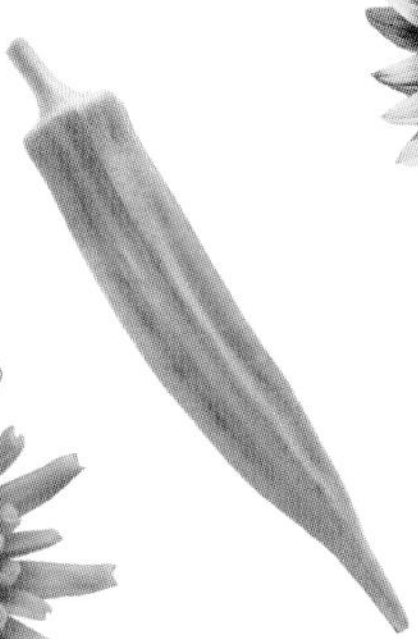
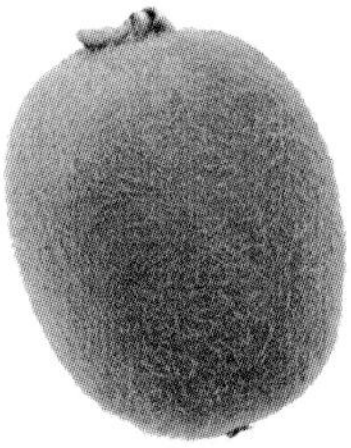
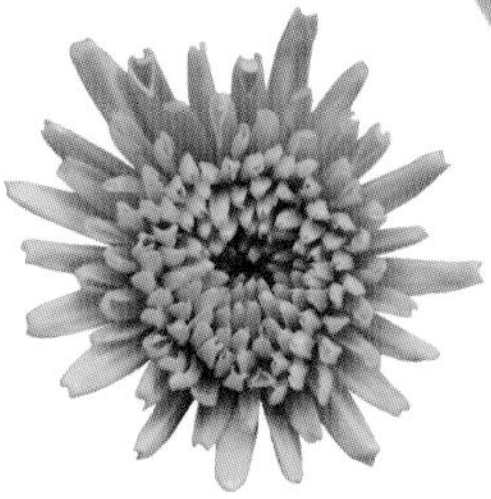
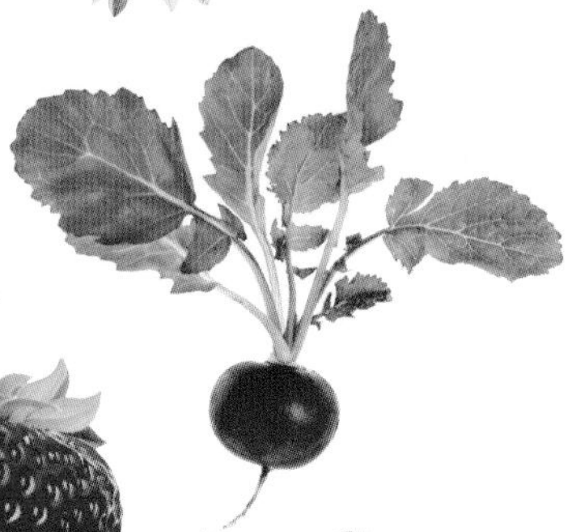
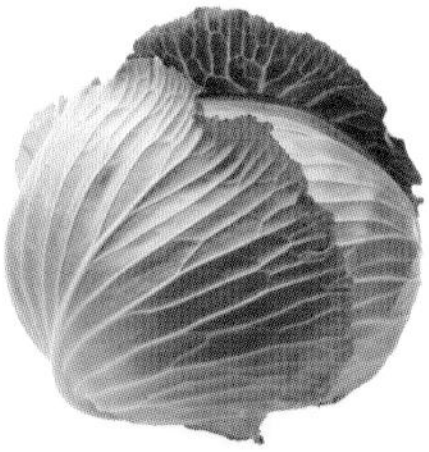
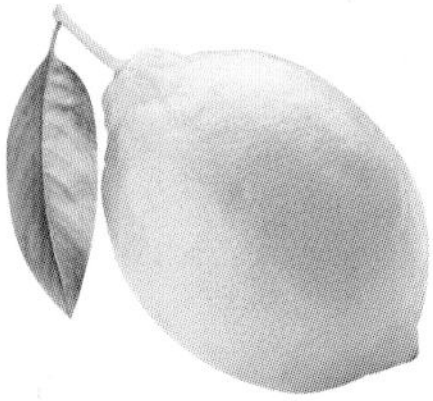
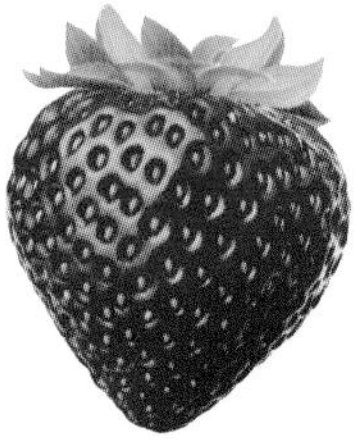
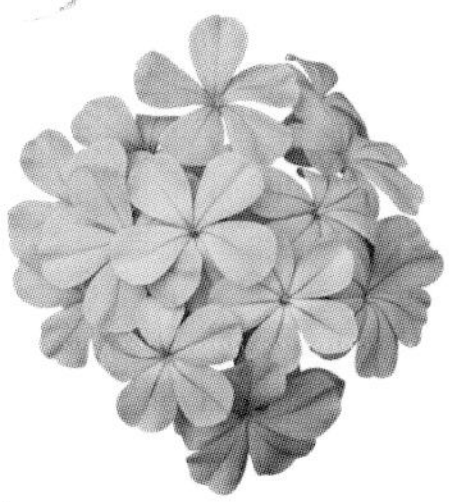
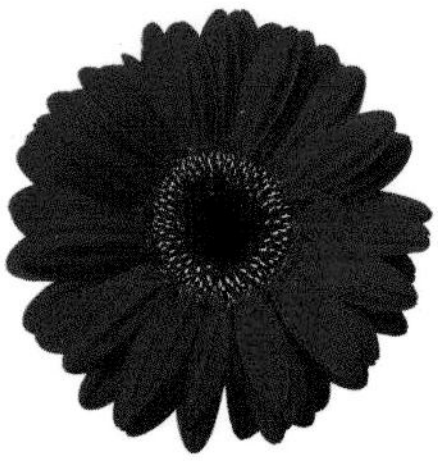
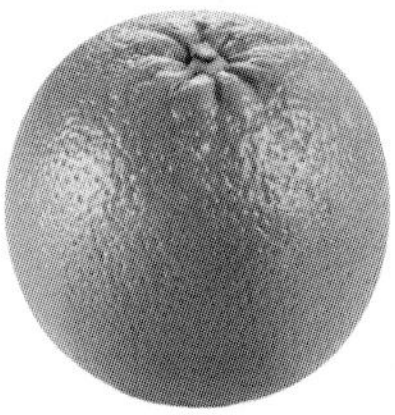
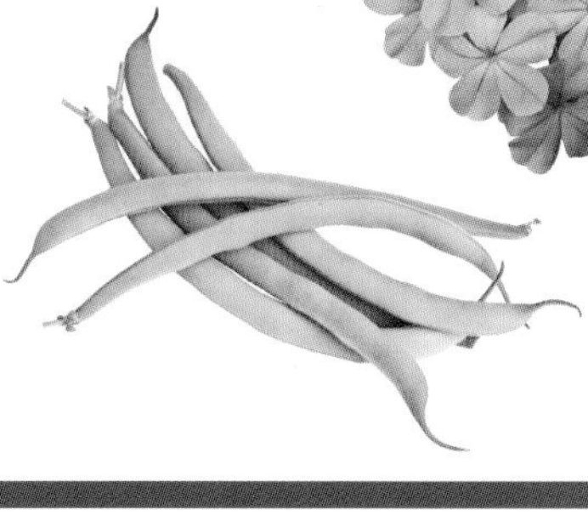

Answers on page 113.

Something's Wrong

What is wrong in this picture? Find 5 mistakes.

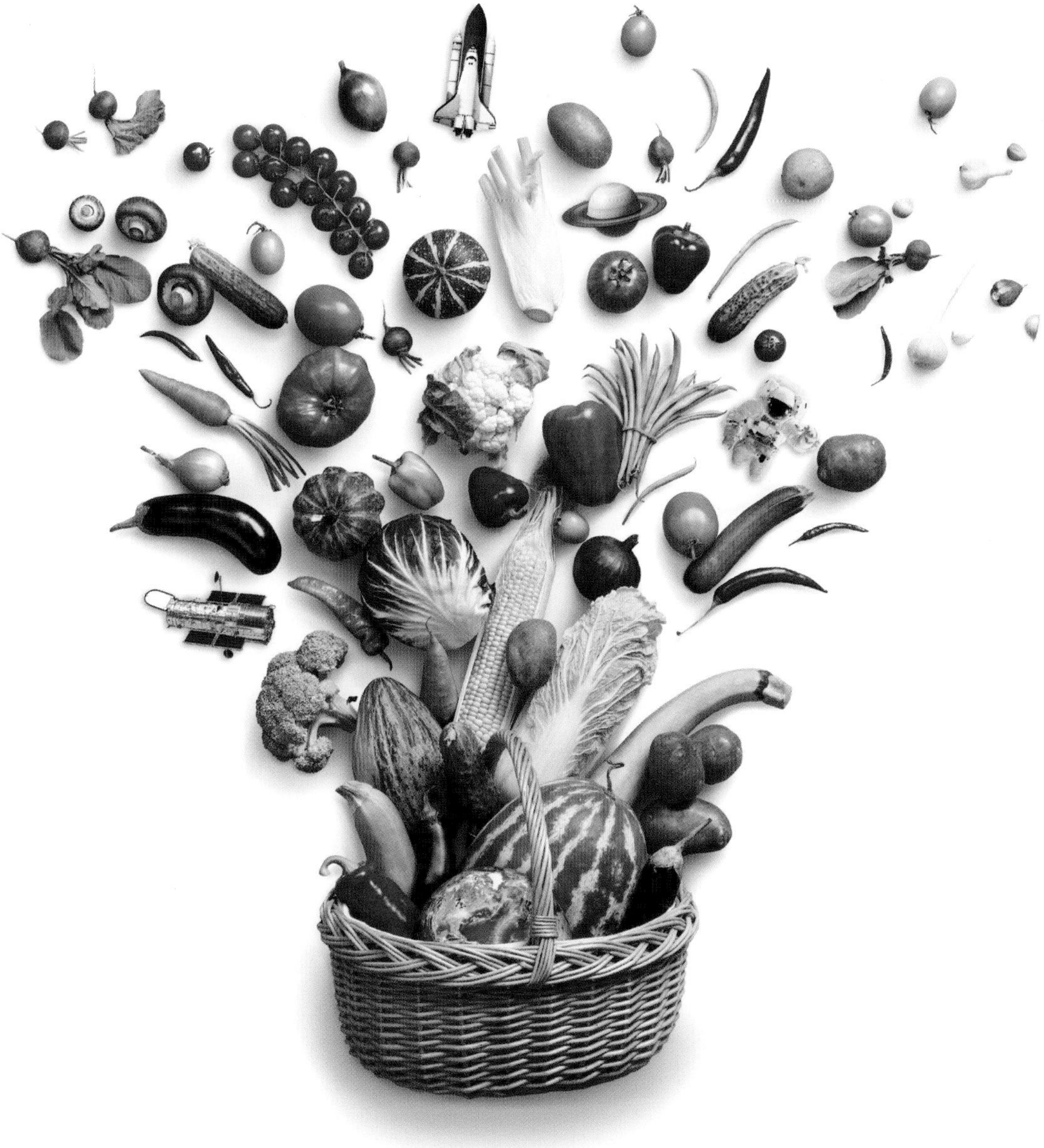

Answers on page 113.

Missing Piece

Circle the piece that goes in the missing spot.

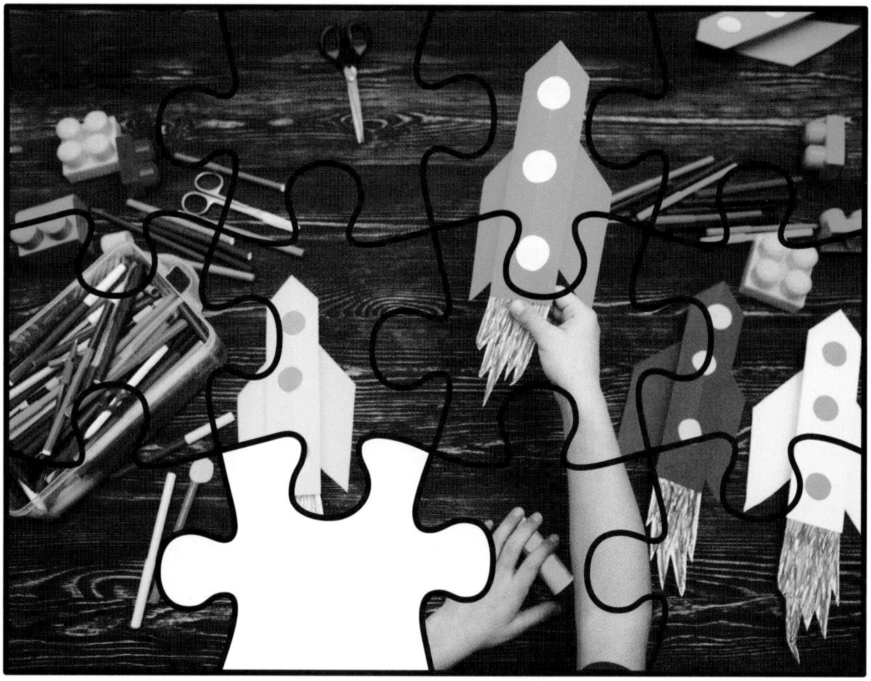

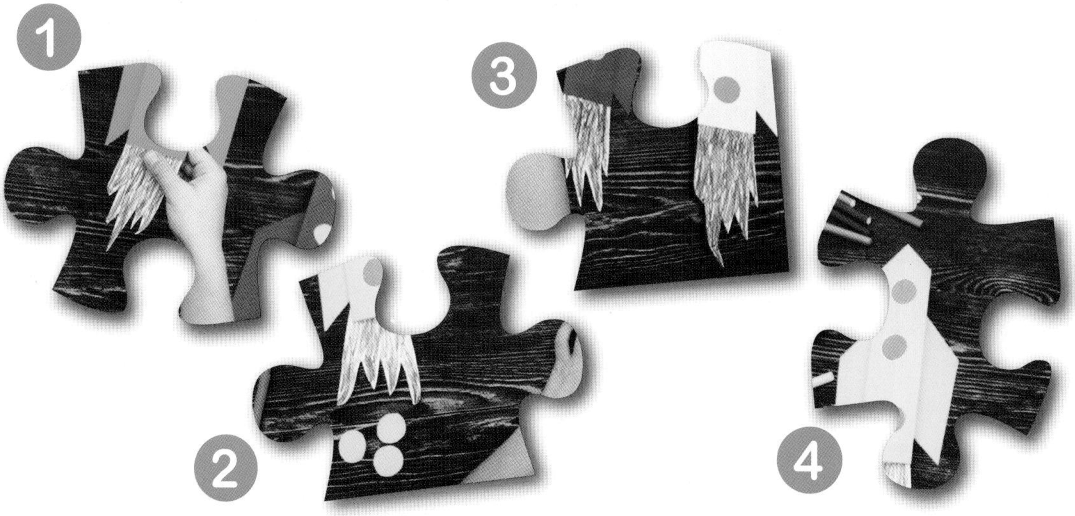
1
2
3
4

Answers on page 113.

Clues

I saw a vehicle today. Use the clues to figure out which vehicle I saw.

The vehicle cannot fly.

The vehicle has 4 wheels.

The vehicle is not yellow.

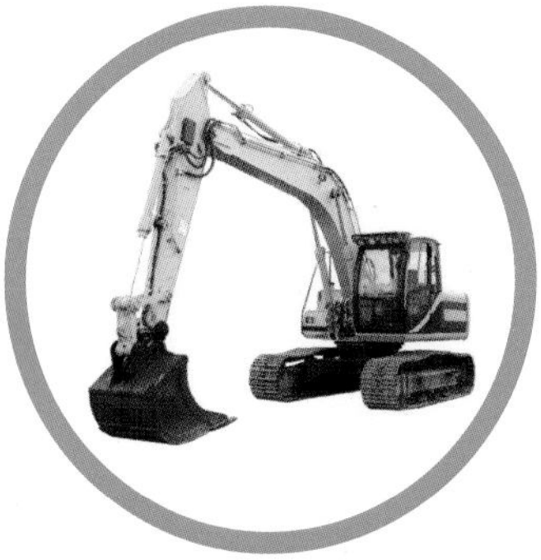

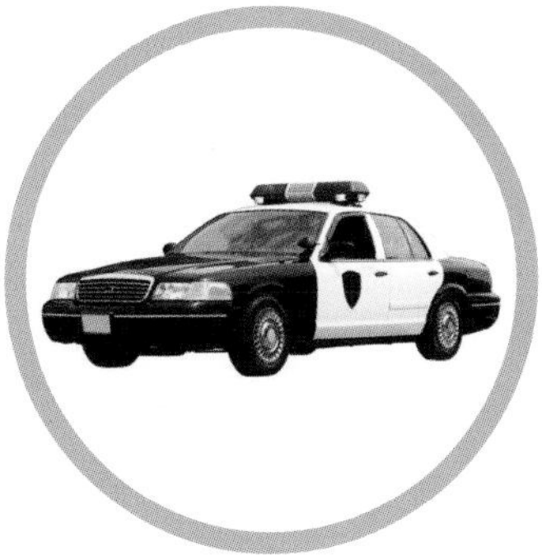

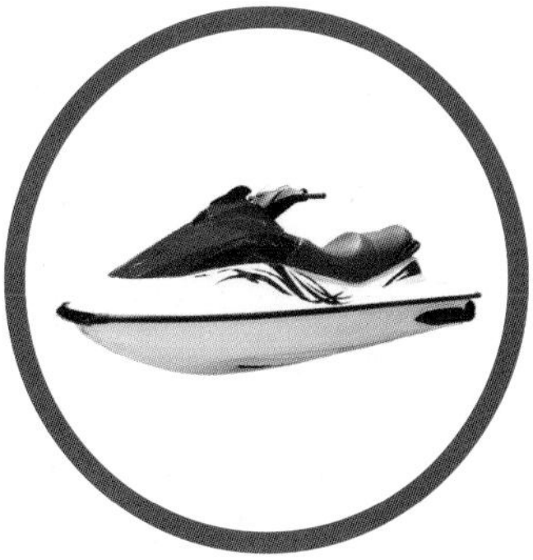

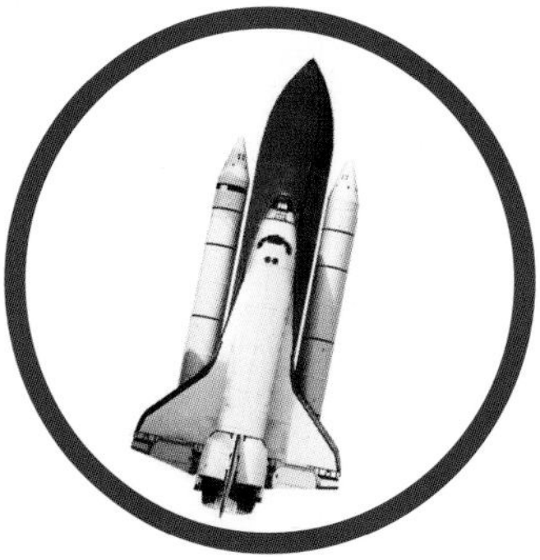

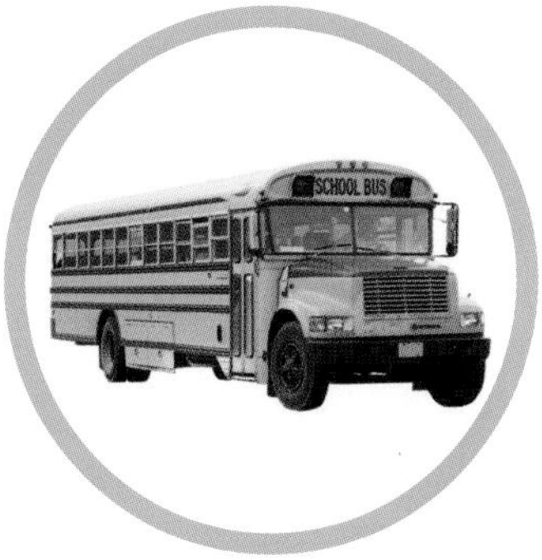
SCHOOL BUS

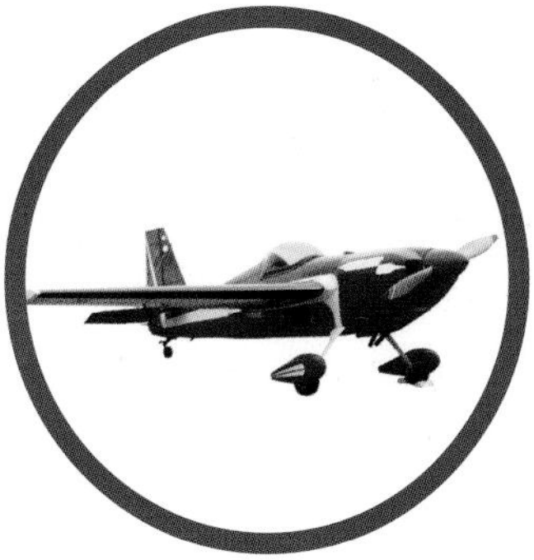

Answers on page 114.

What's Different?

Circle the 6 differences between these pictures.

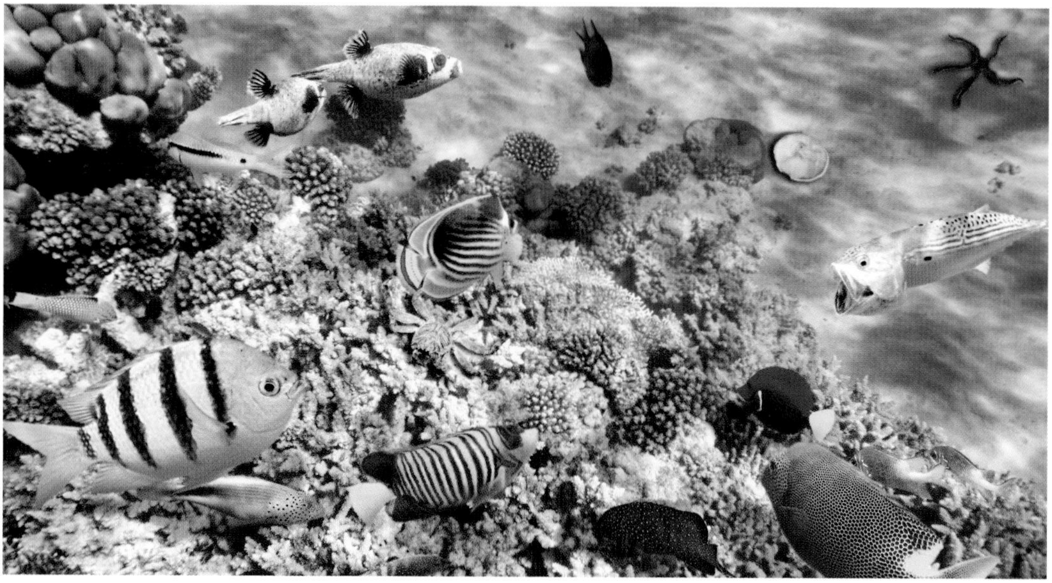

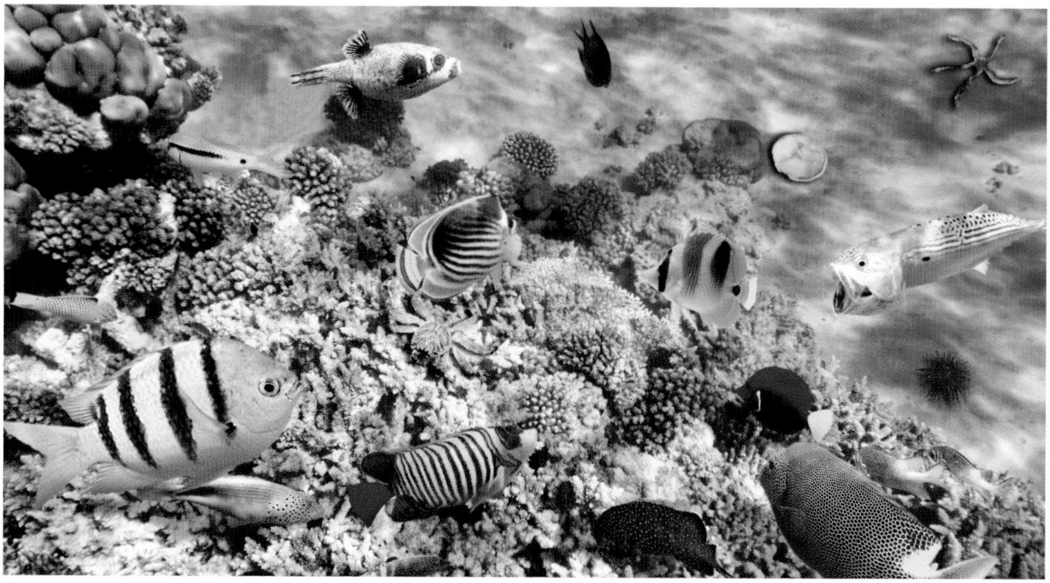

Answers on page 114.

On the Right Path

Follow the path that goes through every farm animal.
But avoid the bears!

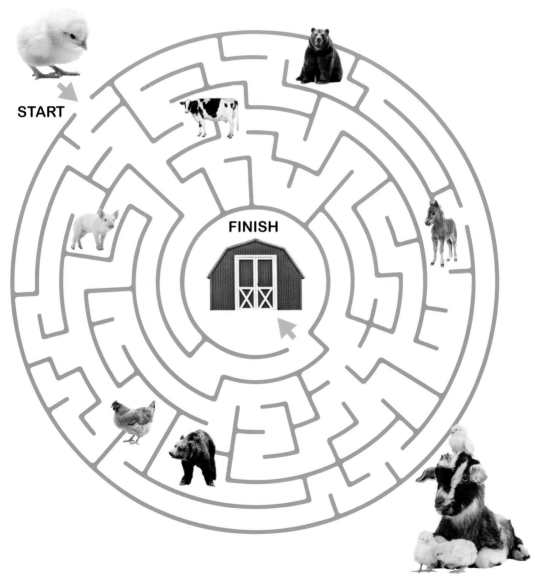

START

FINISH

Hide and Seek

Find the animals hiding around this lake.

1 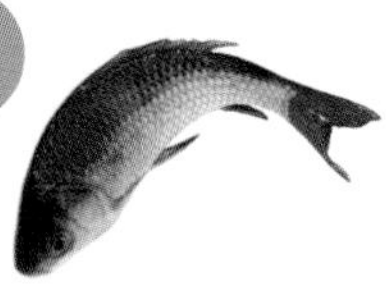 2 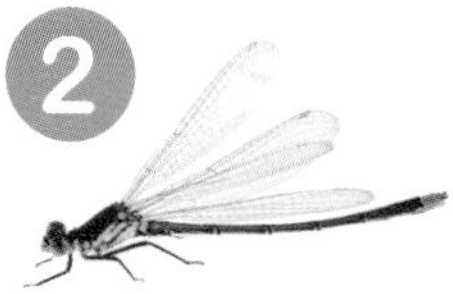 3 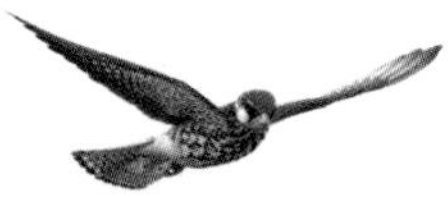 4 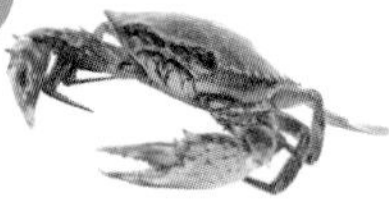

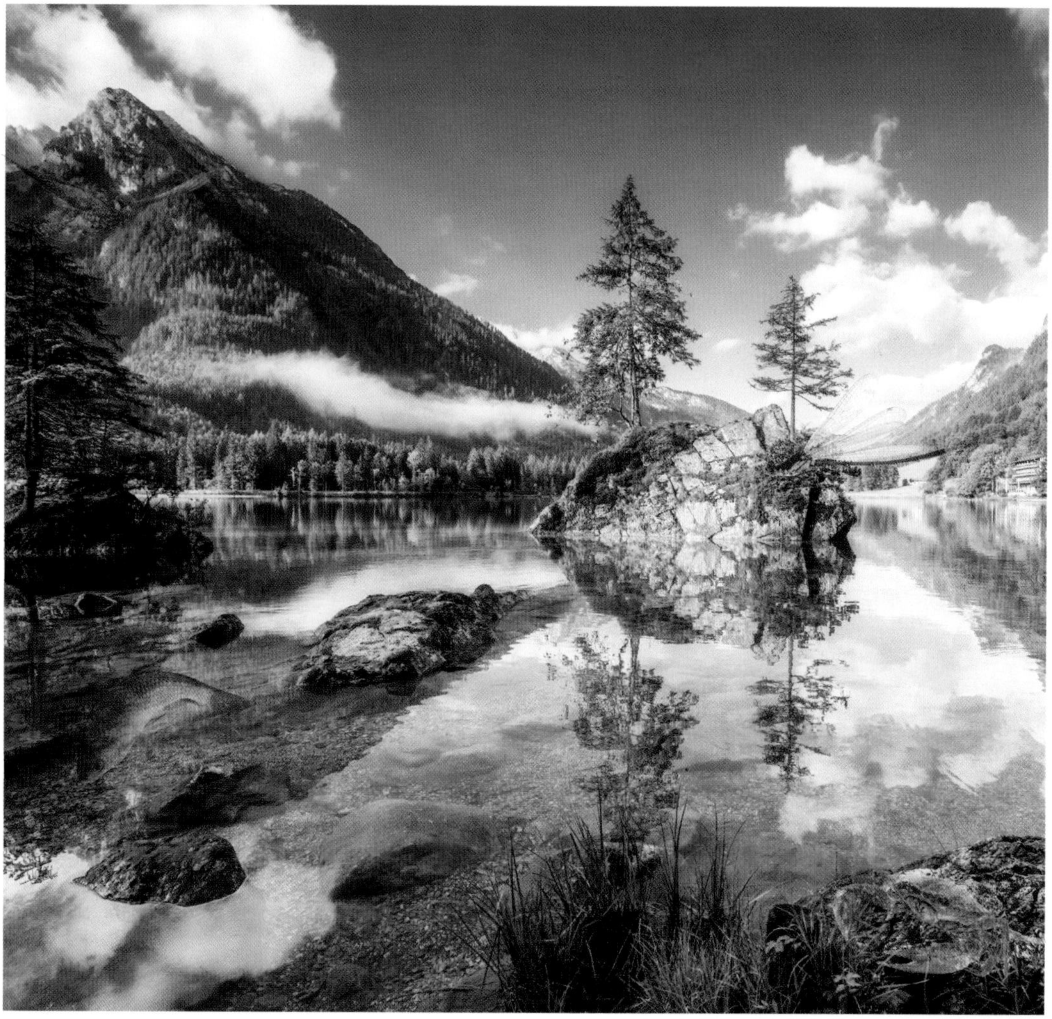

Answers on page 114.

Memory

Look at this picture for 1 minute. Remember as much as you can! Then turn the page.

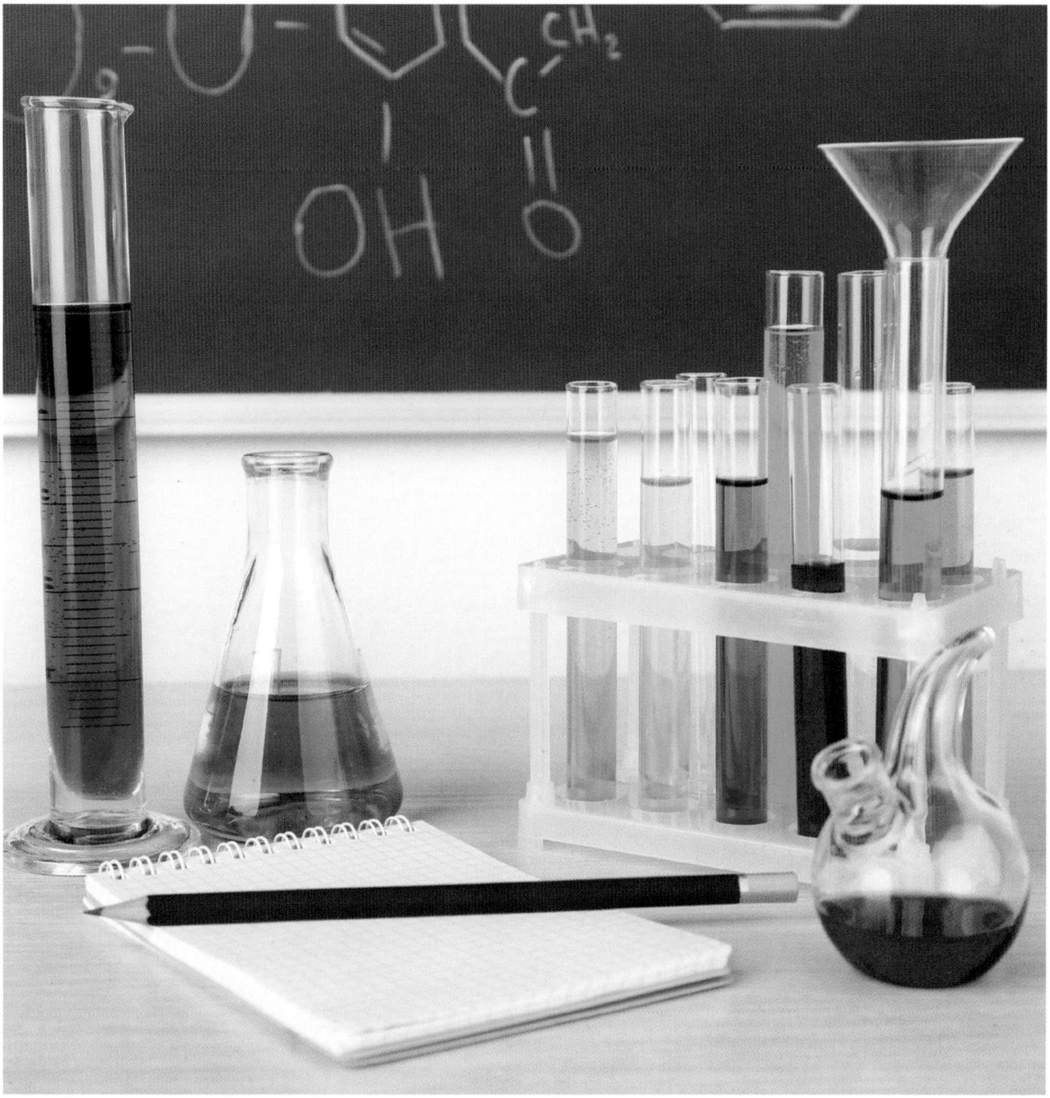
OH

What is different in this picture? Find 3 things that are different.

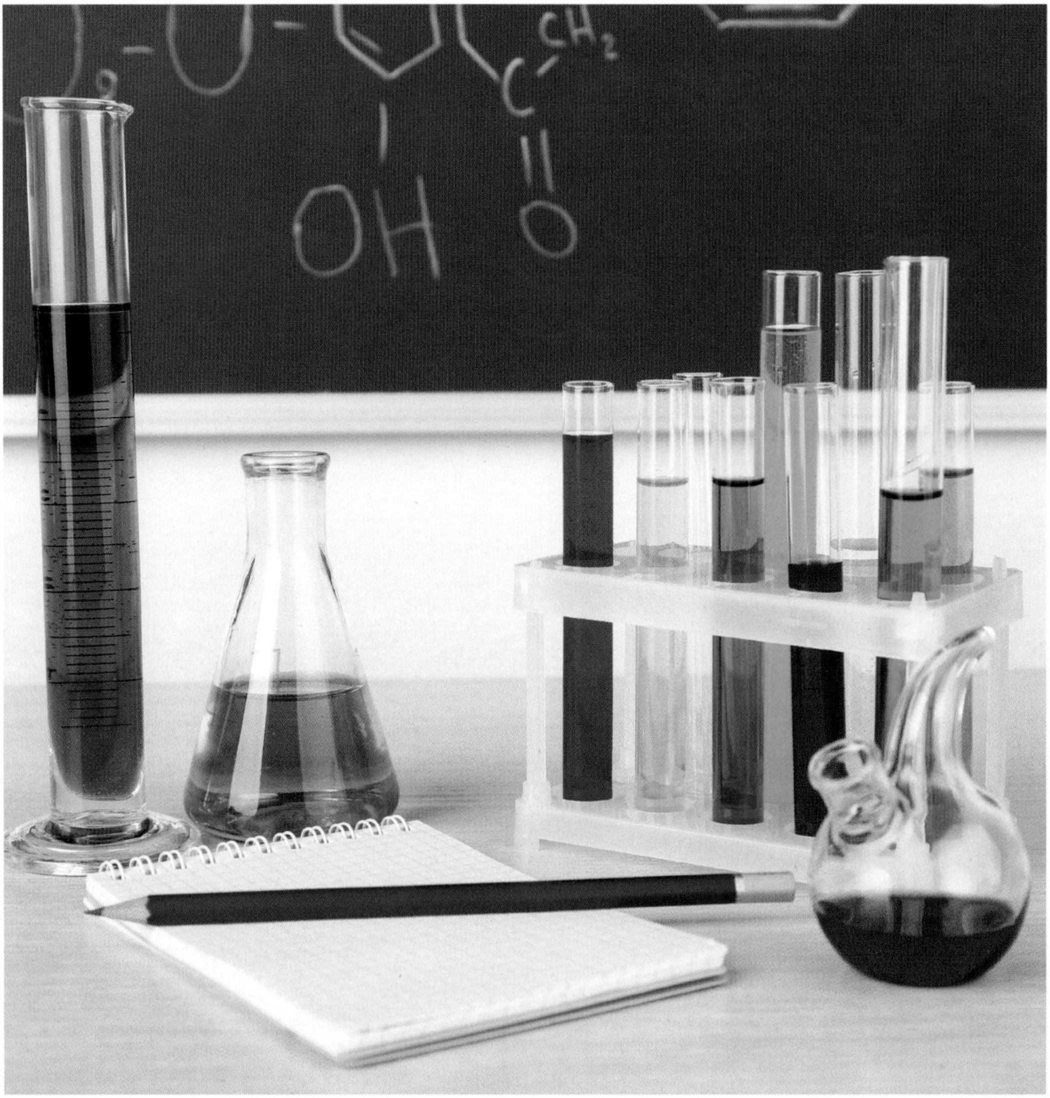
CH2
OH
O

Answers on page 115.

What's Next?

Something is happening to the weather. What will happen next?

Zoom In

Draw a line from each zoomed picture to the object it matches.

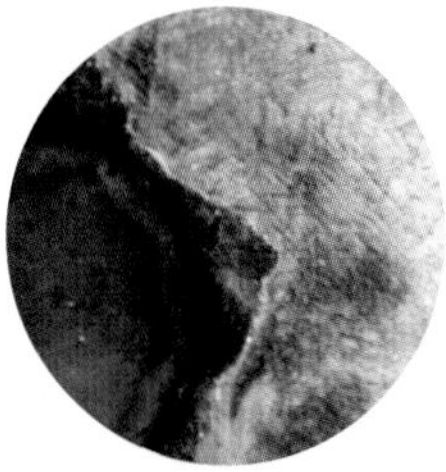

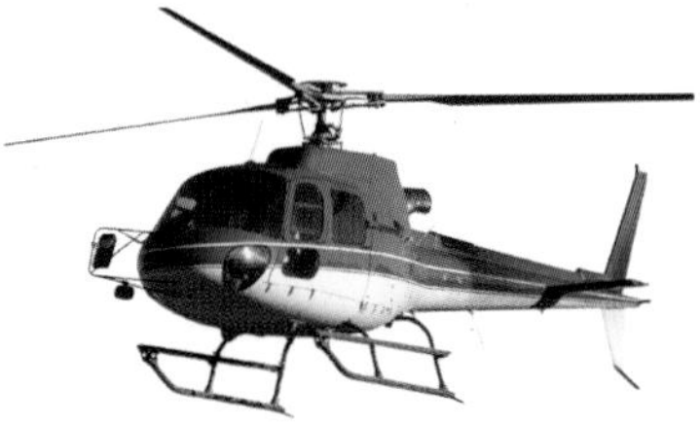

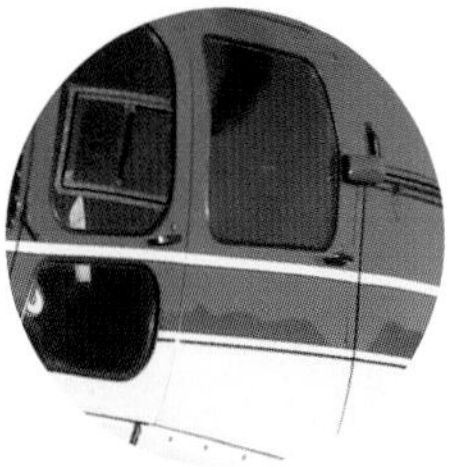

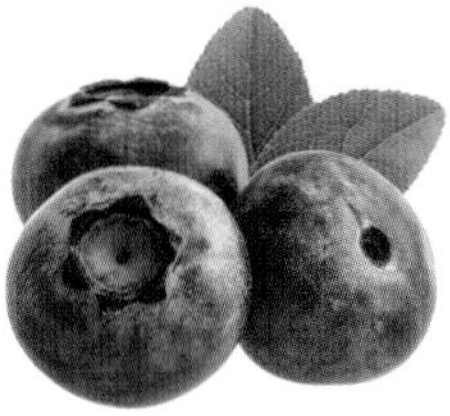

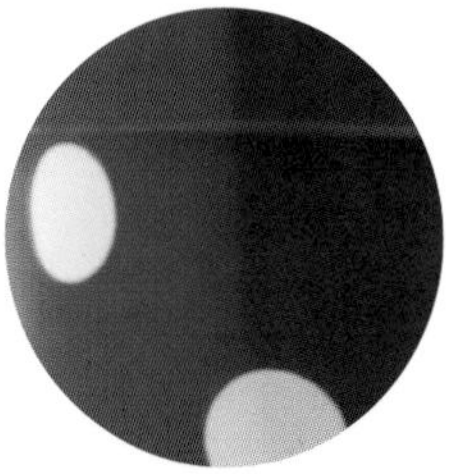

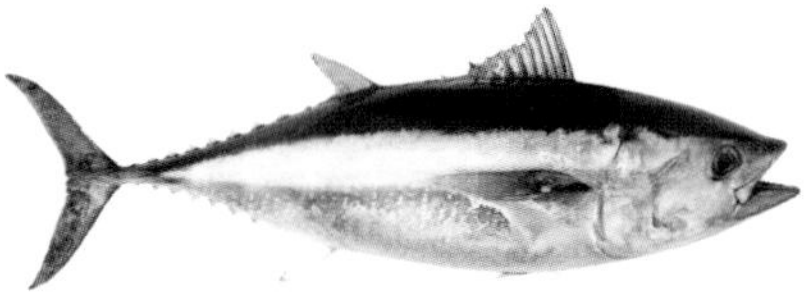

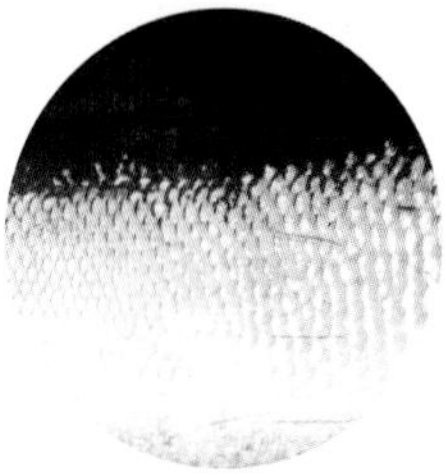

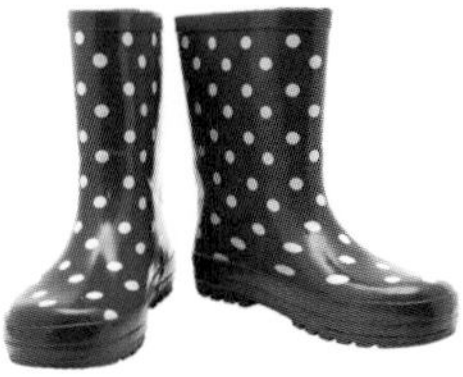

Answers on page 115.

What's Different?

Circle the 6 differences between these pictures.

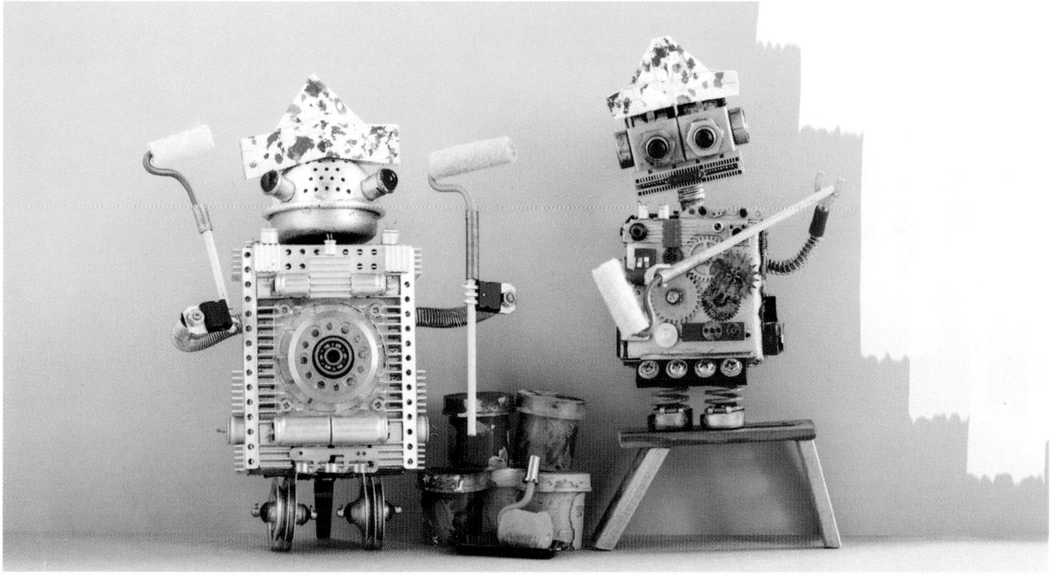

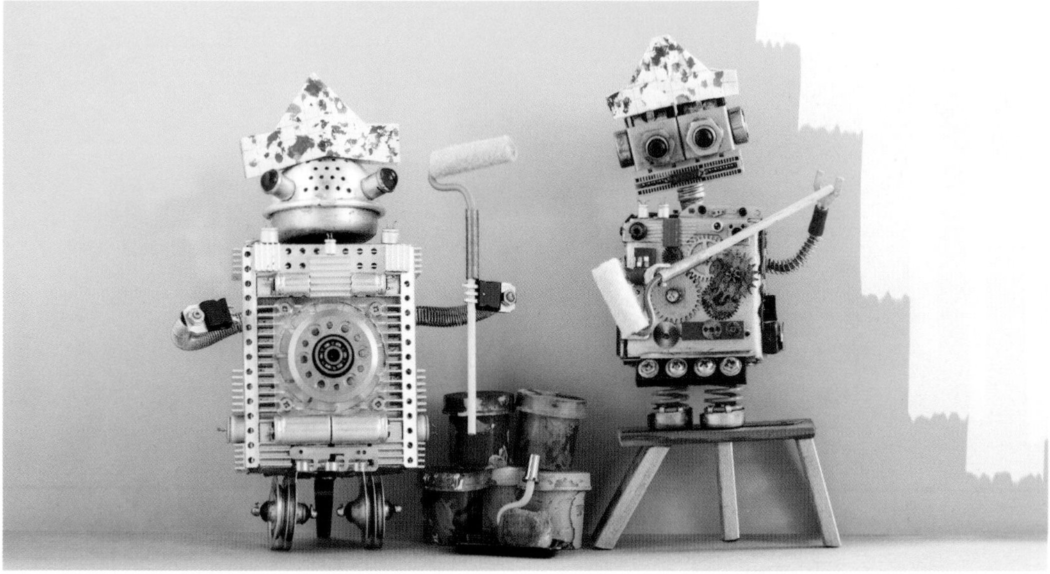

Answers on page 115.

Taste Test

Have you ever eaten while you had a stuffy nose? Did the food taste different? Your tongue is not the only body part that helps you taste food. Your nose does too!

What you need:

- A handful of jelly beans in a variety of flavors (Other candies that come in a variety of flavors will also work)

- A plate

Directions:

1. Put the jelly beans on the plate. With your eyes closed, mix the jelly beans with your hands and spread them apart.

2. Keep your eyes closed. Pinch your nose shut.

3. Pick up one jelly bean and put it in your mouth. What do you taste? What kind jelly bean do you think it is?

4. Start to chew it, keeping your eyes and nose closed. What do you taste now? Has your guess about the candy's flavor changed?

5. Let go of your nose so you can breathe through it again. Has the taste changed? What kind do you think it is now?

6. Repeat steps 2 through 5 with a few more jelly beans.

How many of your guesses were correct?

Extra challenge!

Try this activity with a friend. See who can guess the right flavor more times.

Answers on page 116.

47

Something's Wrong

What is wrong in this picture? Find 5 mistakes.

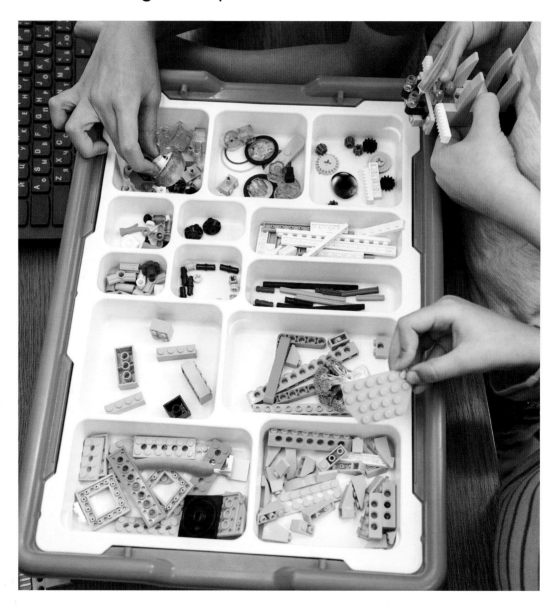

Answers on page 116.

What Do I Do?

What am I? What do I help people do?

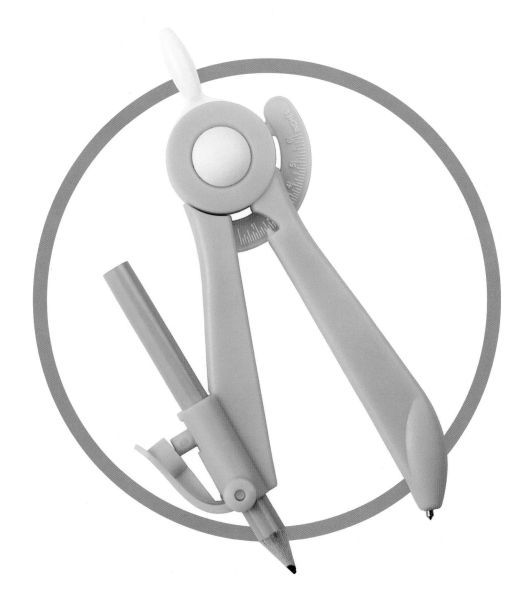

Answers on page 116.

Out of Order

These pictures are in the wrong order! What is the right order?

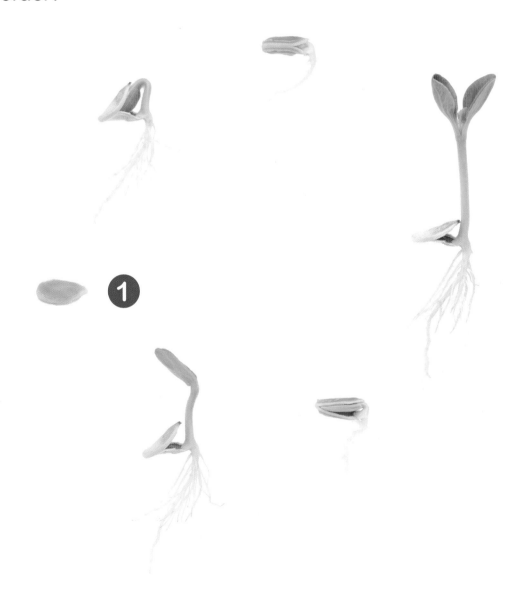

50

Answers on page 116.

Match It

Draw a line to connect each animal to the first letter of its name.

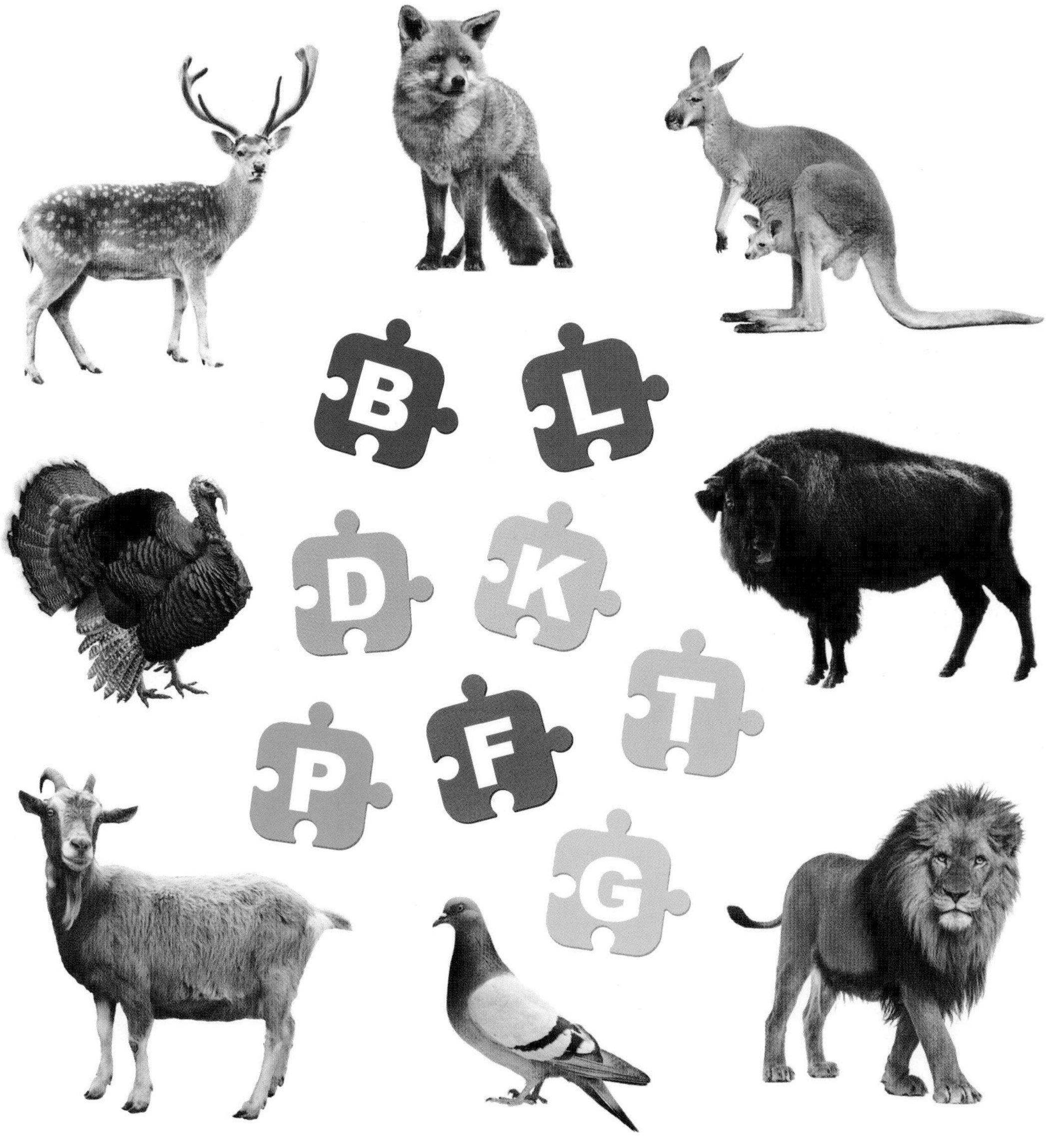
B
L
D
K
P
F
T
G

Answers on page 117.

Where Am I?

Point to the parts of the parrot.

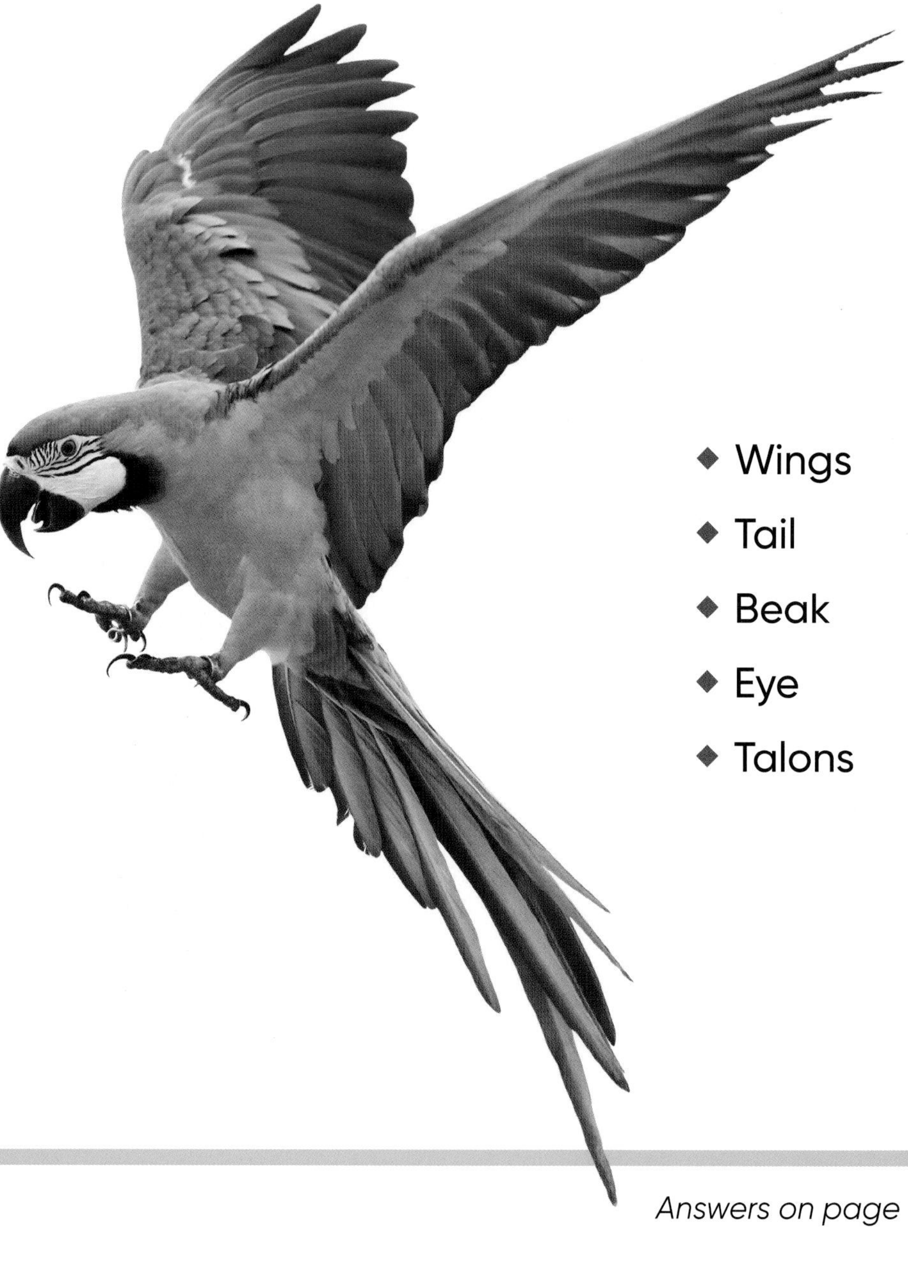

- Wings
- Tail
- Beak
- Eye
- Talons

Answers on page 117.

Do It

Blow on the page. What do you think will happen?
Turn the page to find out.

What happened?

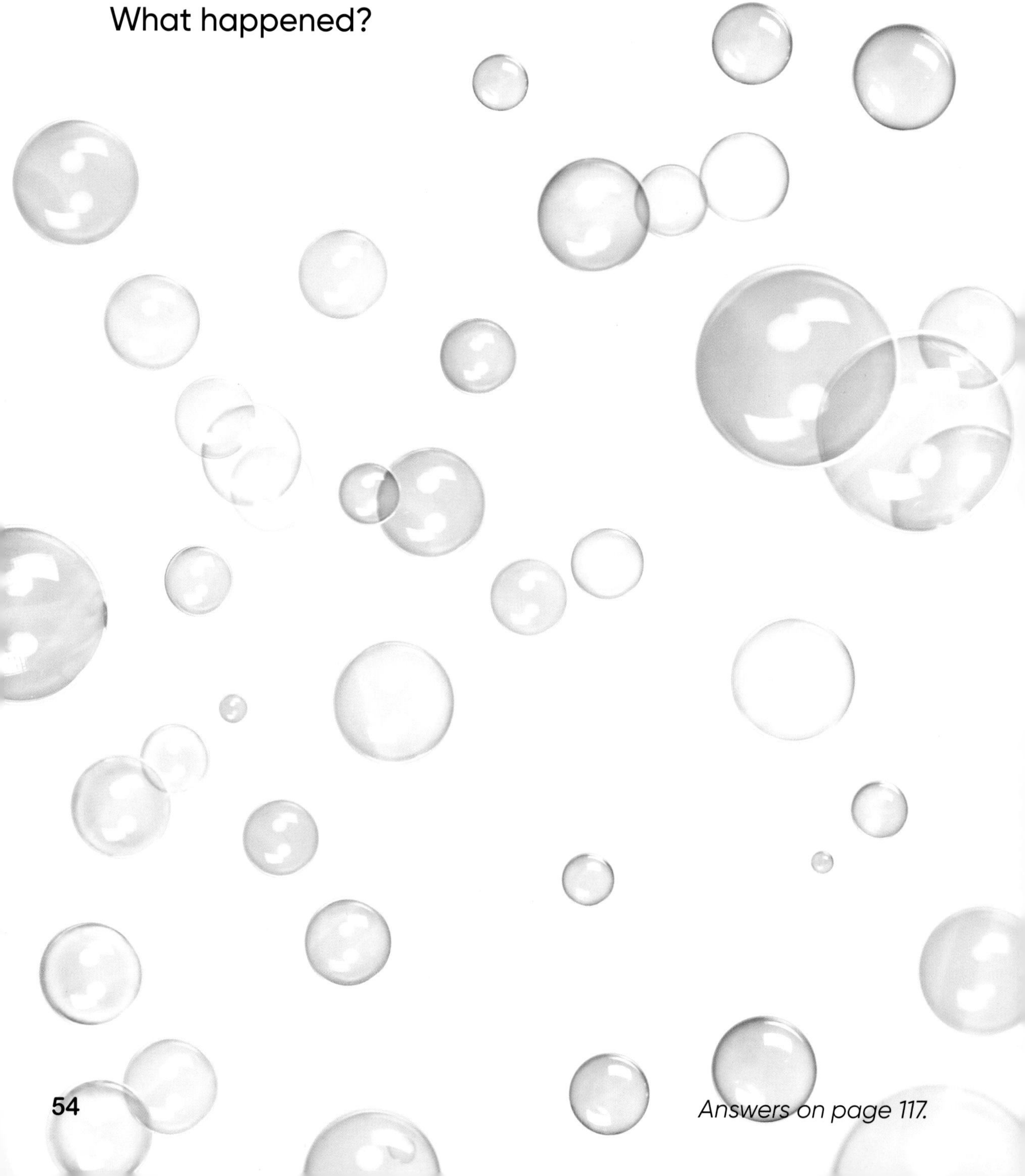

Answers on page 117.

Shadows

Circle the shadow that matches the beetle.

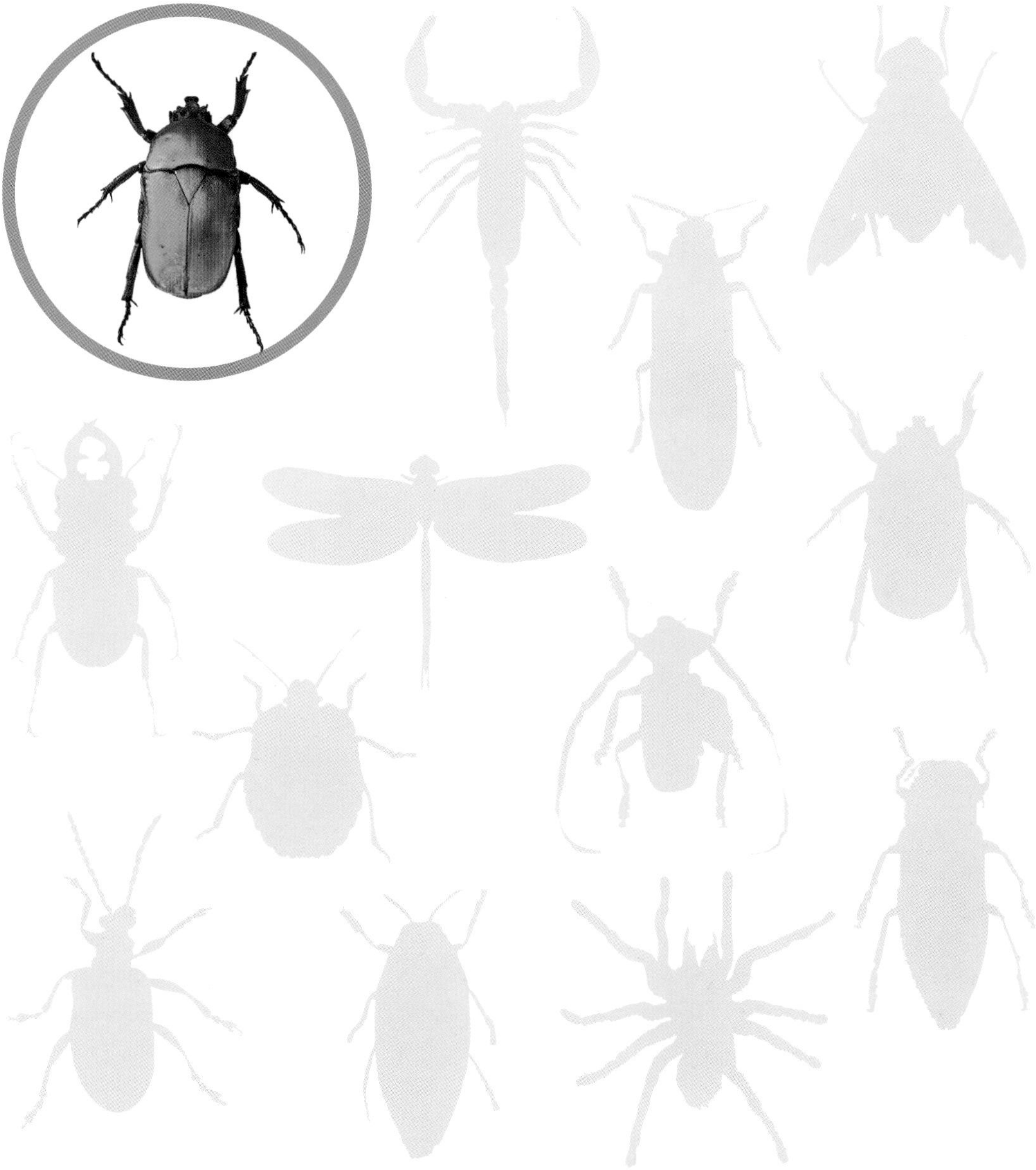

Answers on page 117.

Missing Piece

Circle the piece that goes in the missing spot.

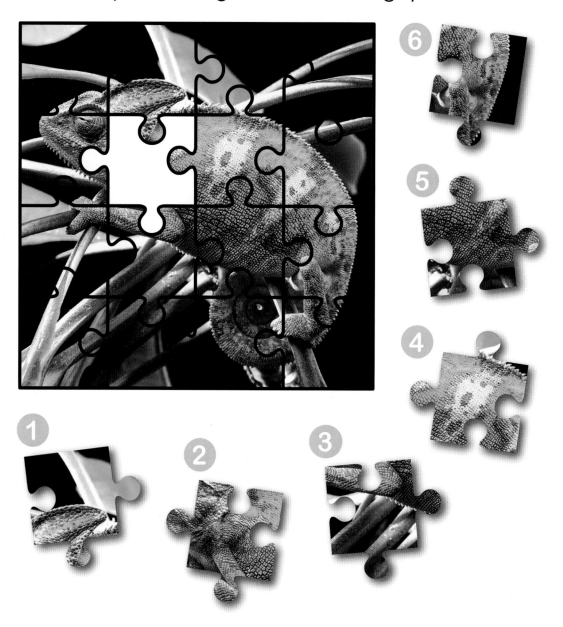

Answers on page 118.

Draw It

The crab is missing its claws and legs! Can you draw the missing parts?

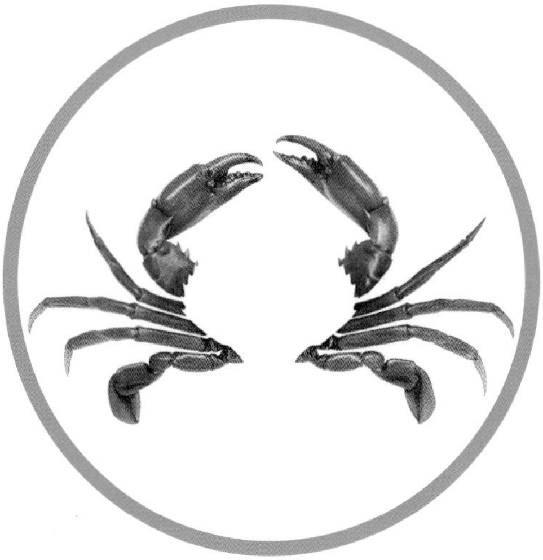

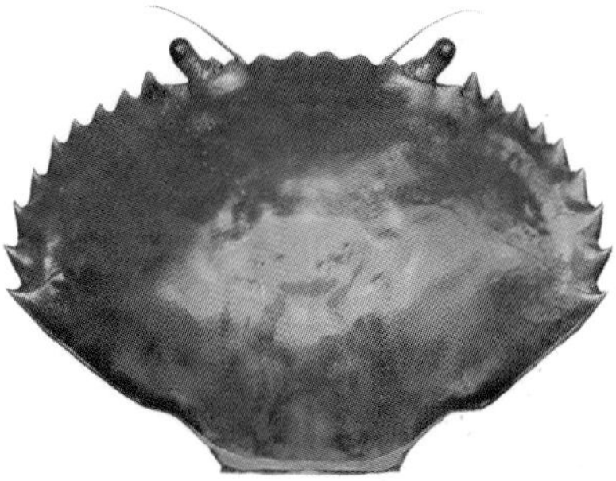

Answers on page 118.

On the Right Path

Follow the path that goes through every pie ingredient.
But avoid the ants!

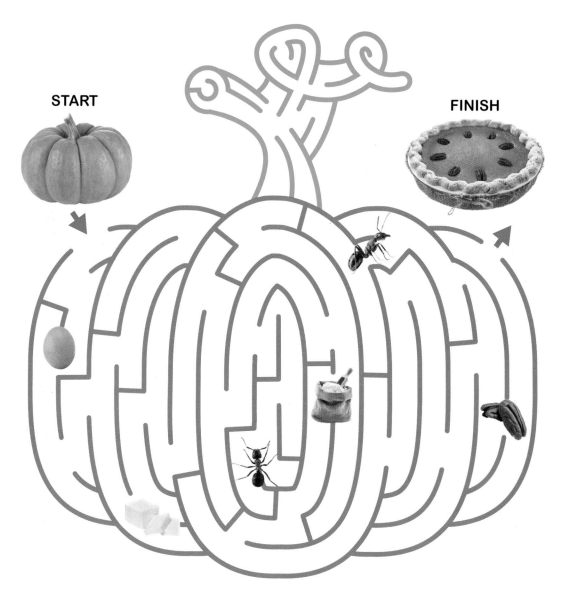

START

FINISH

58

Answers on page 118.

Memory

Look at this picture for 1 minute. Remember as much as you can! Then turn the page.

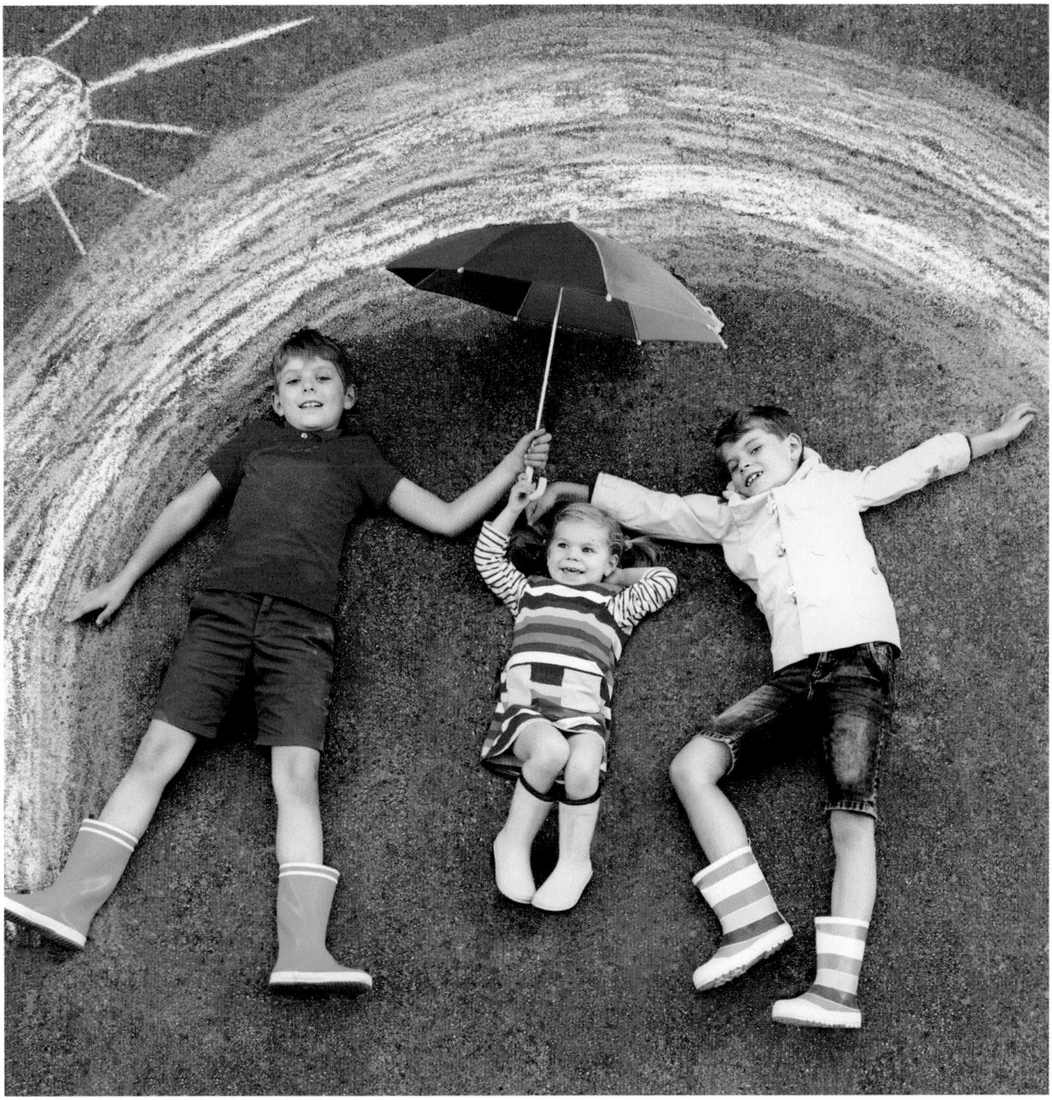

What is different in this picture? Find 4 things that are different.

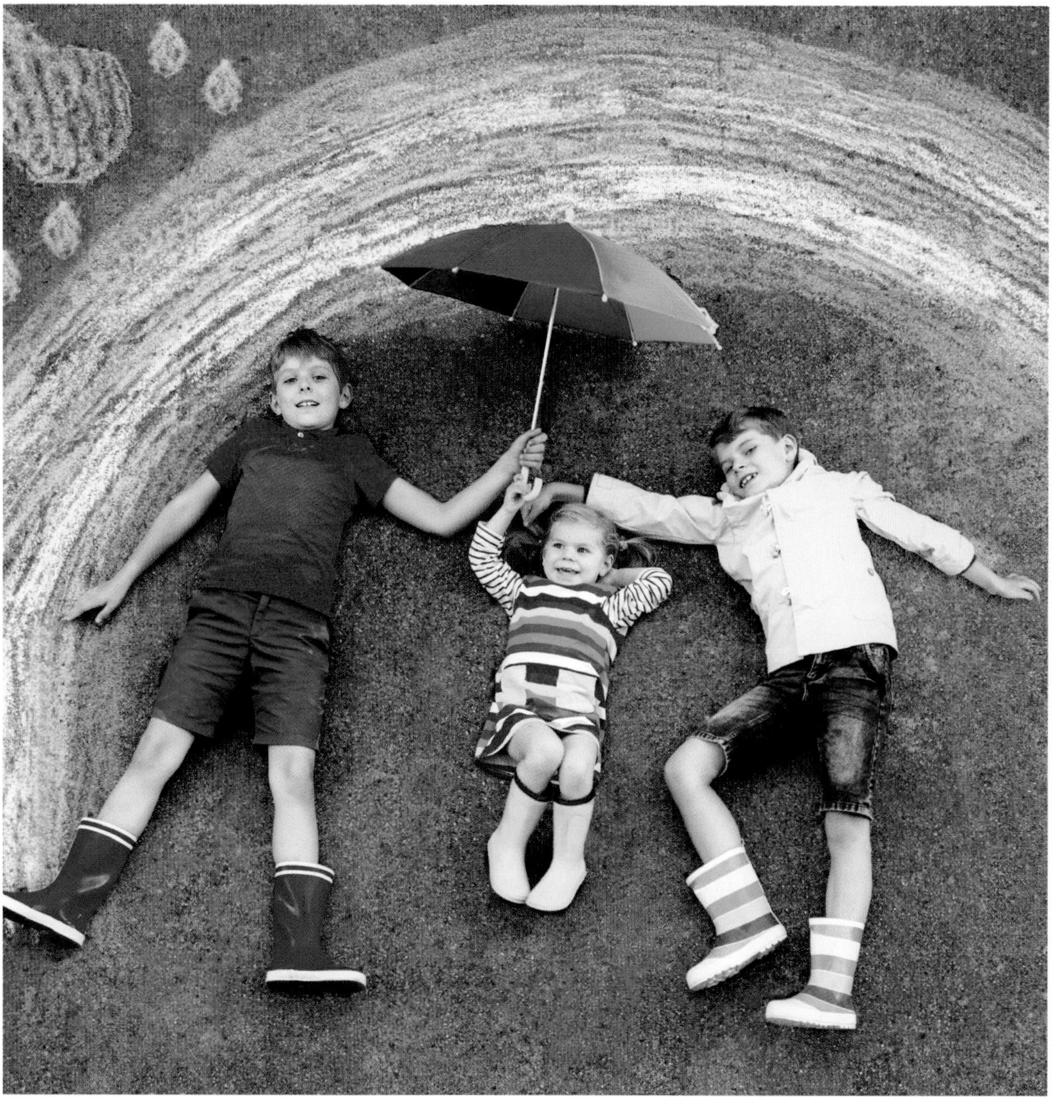

Answers on page 118.

Hide and Seek

Find the animals and vegetable hiding in the garden.

1 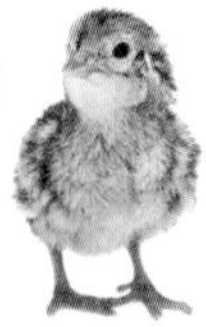 2 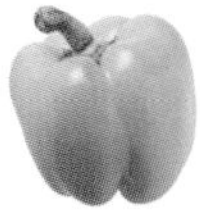 3 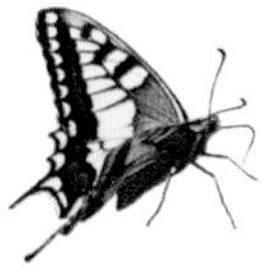 4 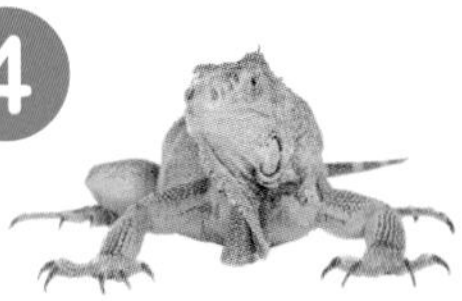

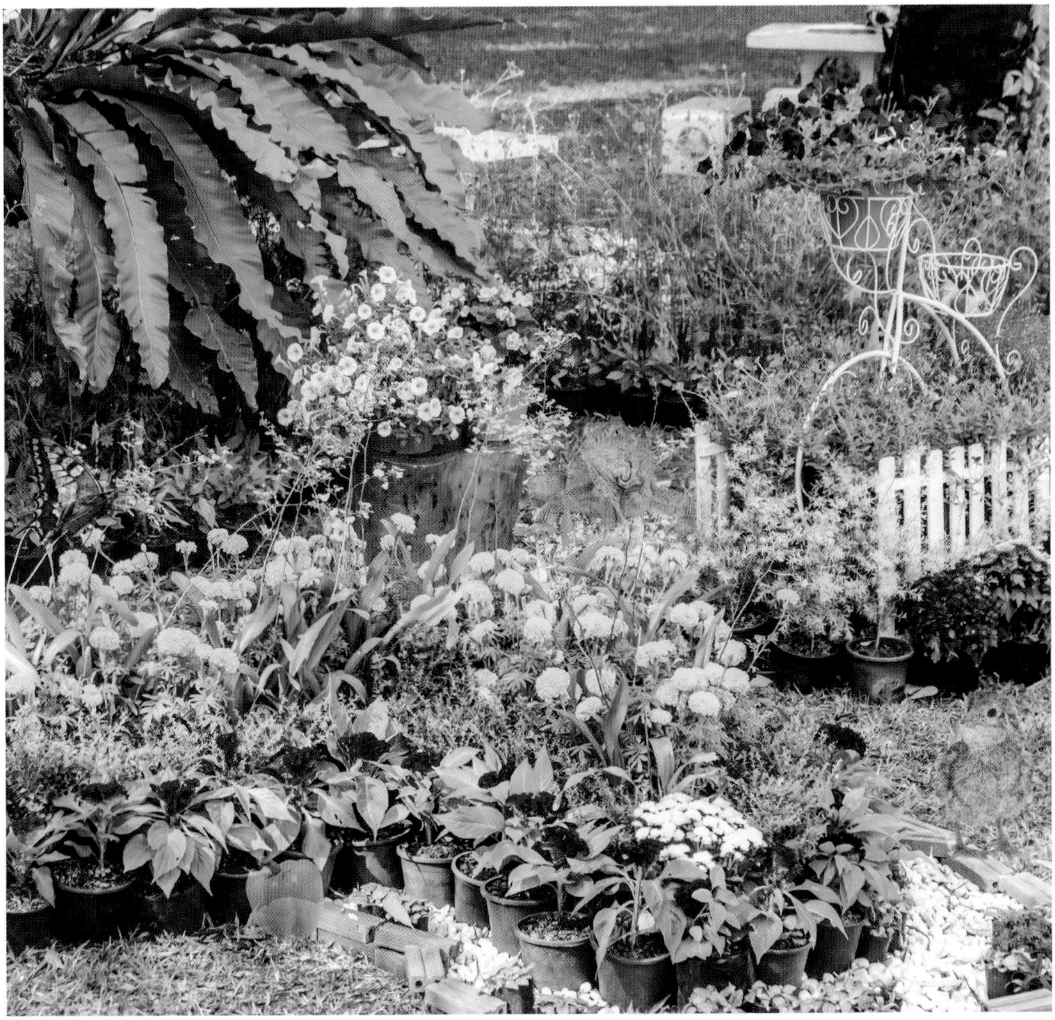

Answers on page 119.

What Is It?

These objects are all cut up! Can you see what each one is?

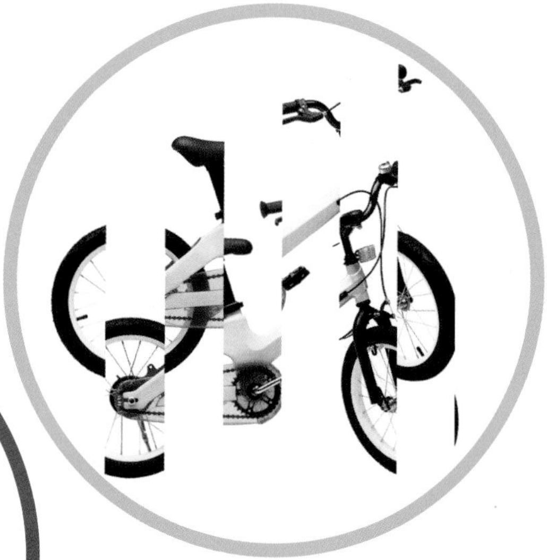

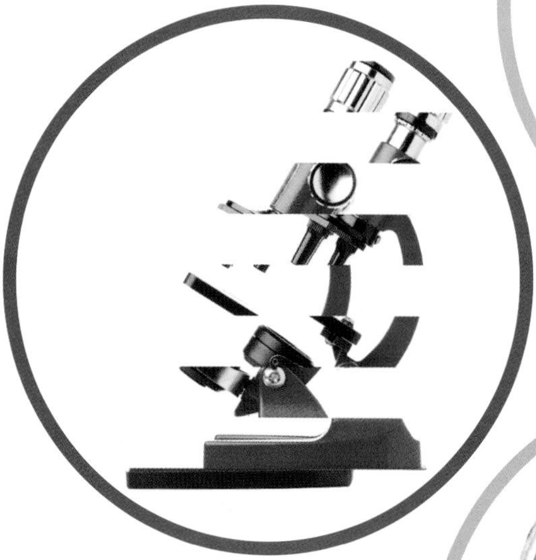

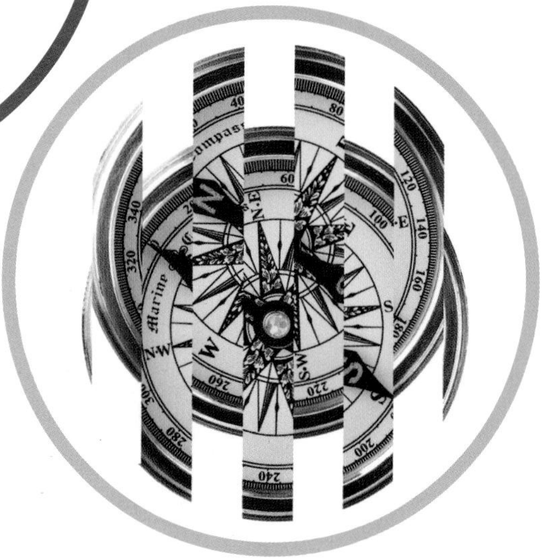

Answers on page 119.

Zoom In

Draw a line from each zoomed picture to the object it matches.

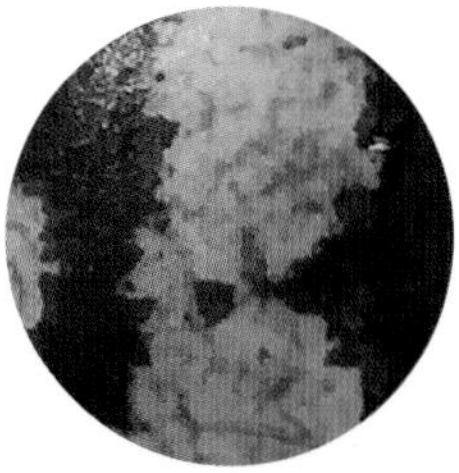

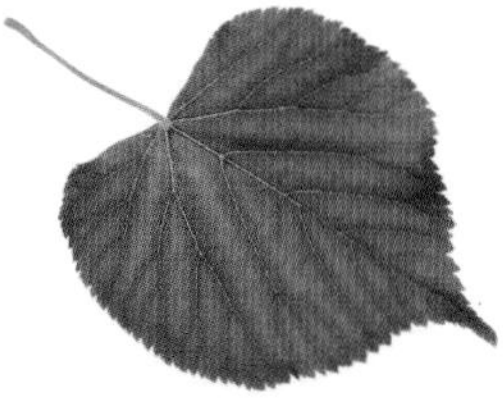

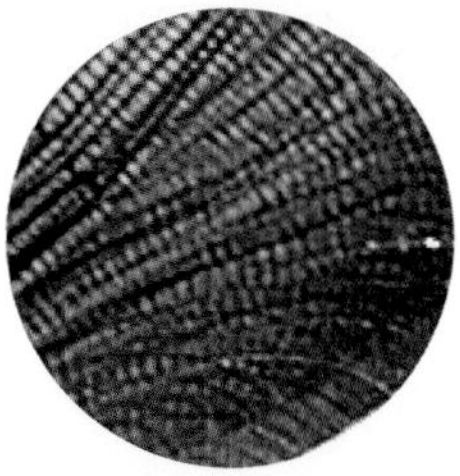

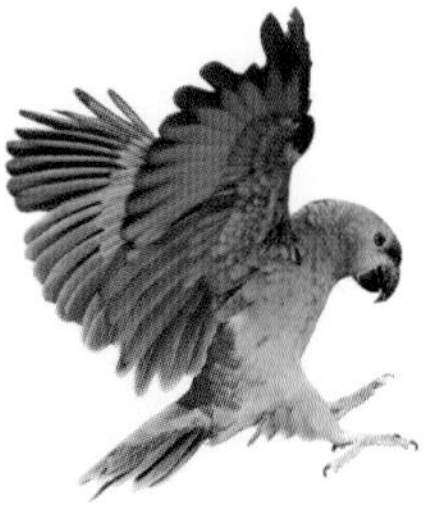

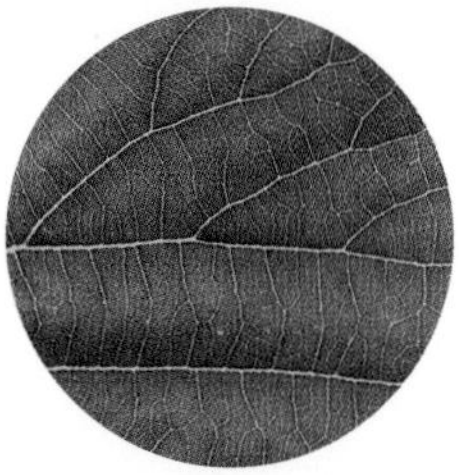

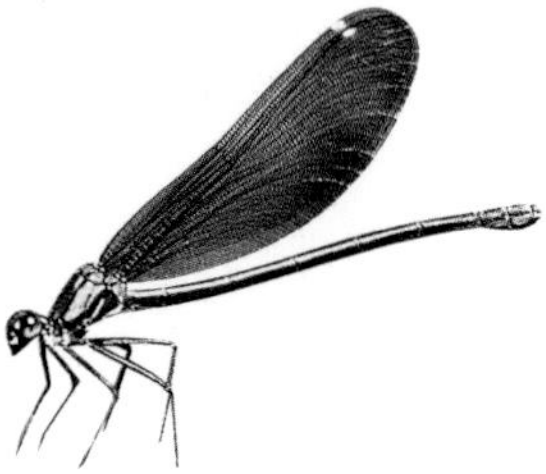

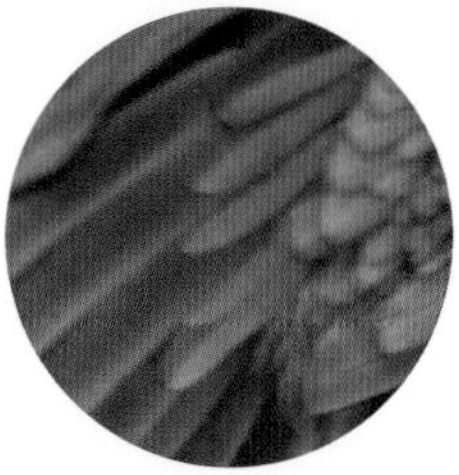

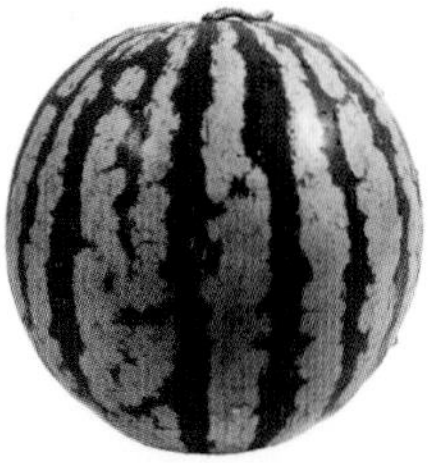

Answers on page 119.

Which Ones?

Circle all of the objects that are used to measure.

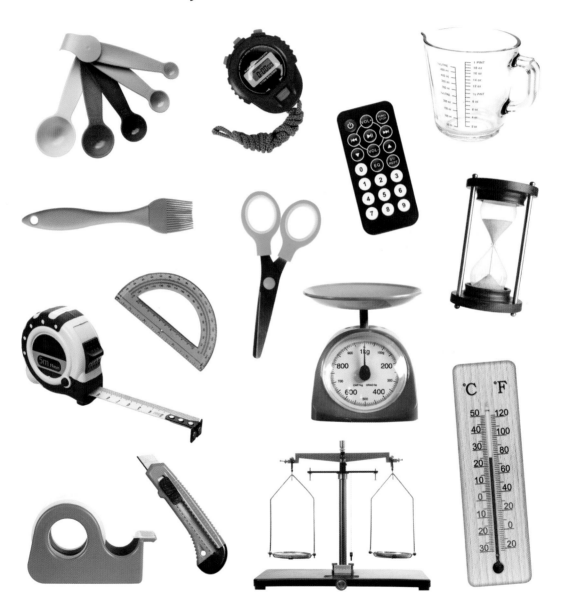

Answers on page 119.

Shadows

Circle the shadow that matches the light bulb.

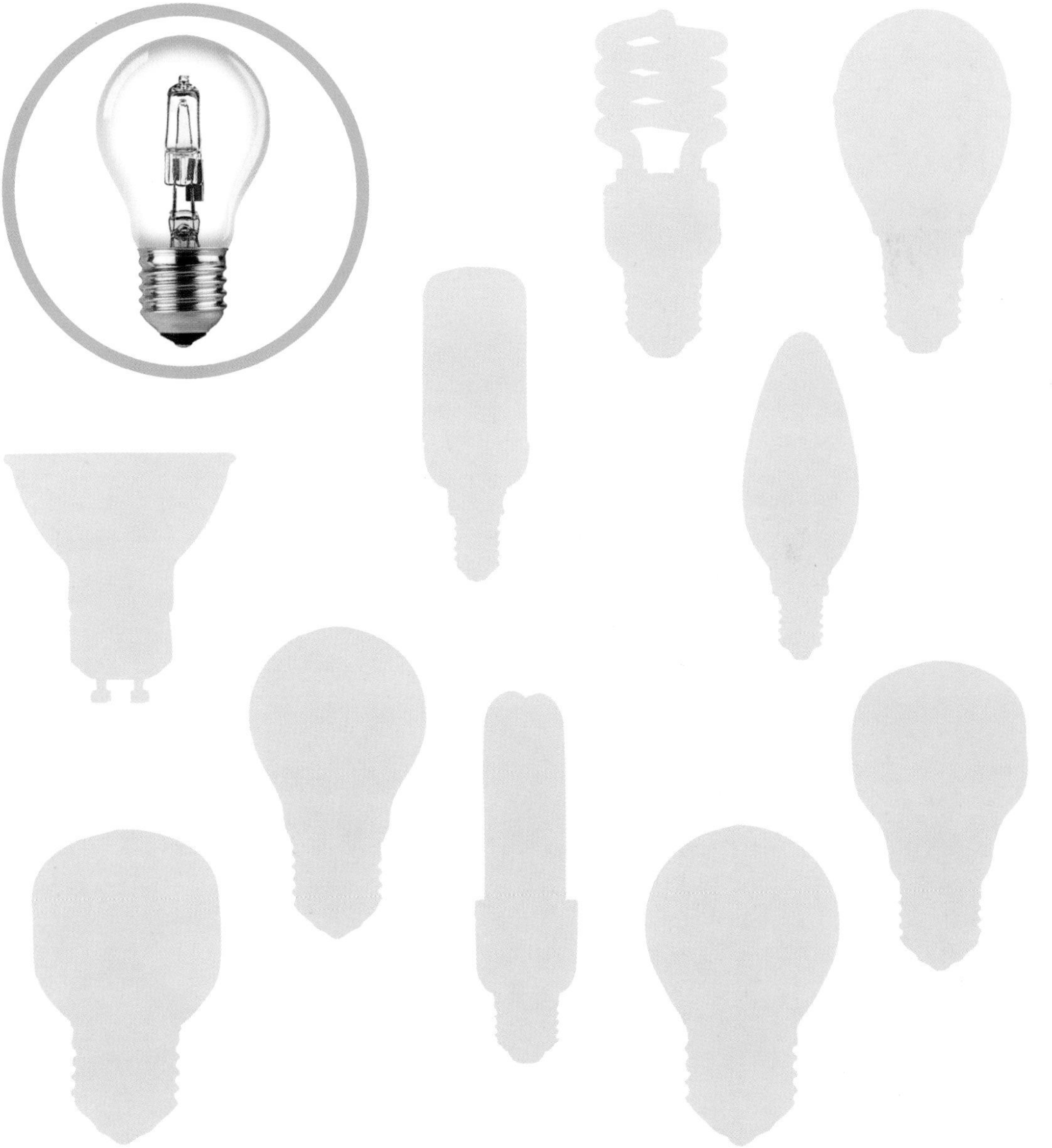

Answers on page 120.

Groups

Write the number of animals that fit in each group. Some might fit in more than one group!

Are mammals? ________

Can fly? ________

Are reptiles? ________

Have fur? ________

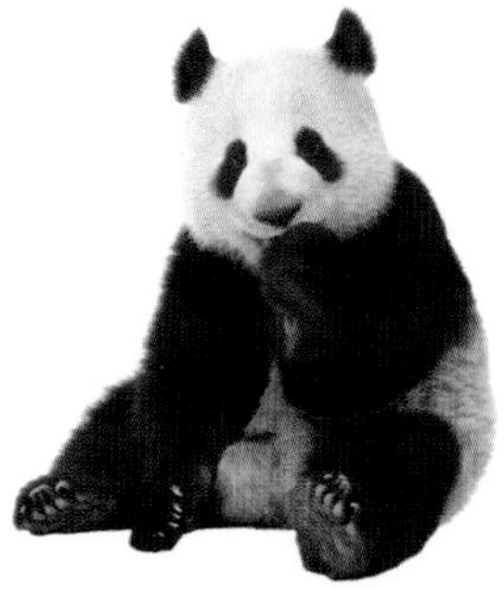

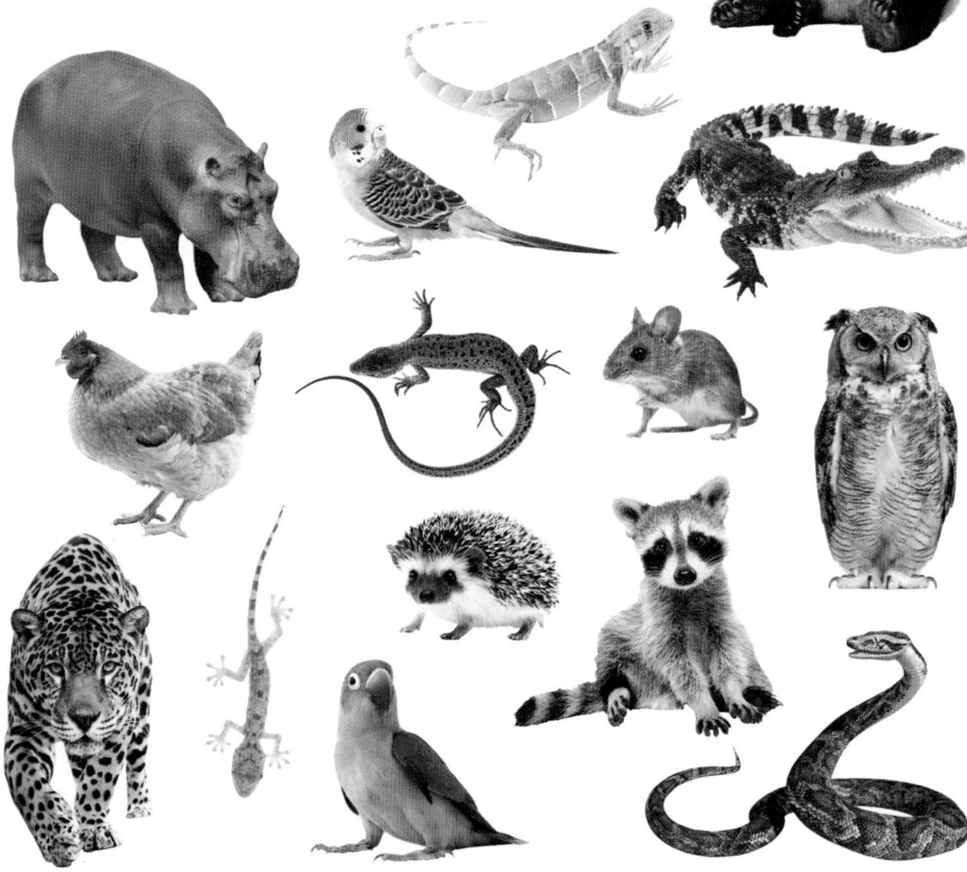

Answers on page 120.

Clues

I saw a sea creature today. Use the clues to figure out which creature I saw.

The creature is not a mammal.

The creature has fins.

The creature can fit in a fish bowl.

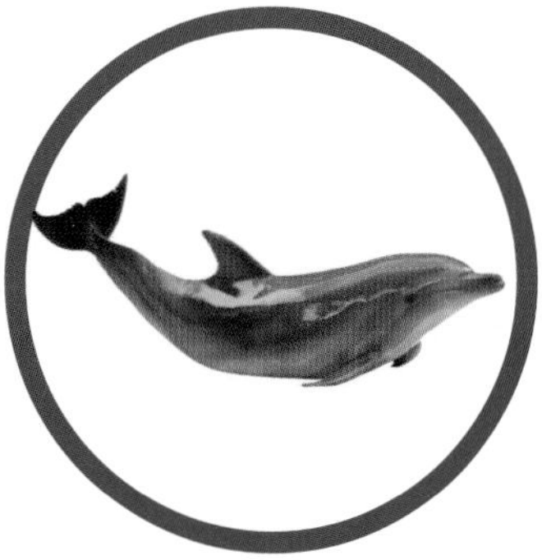
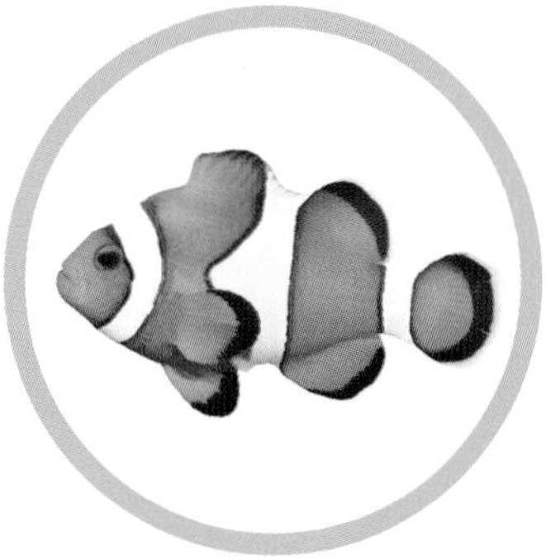
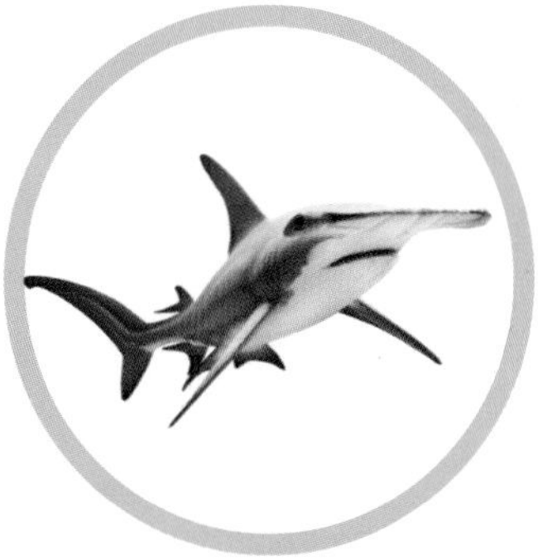
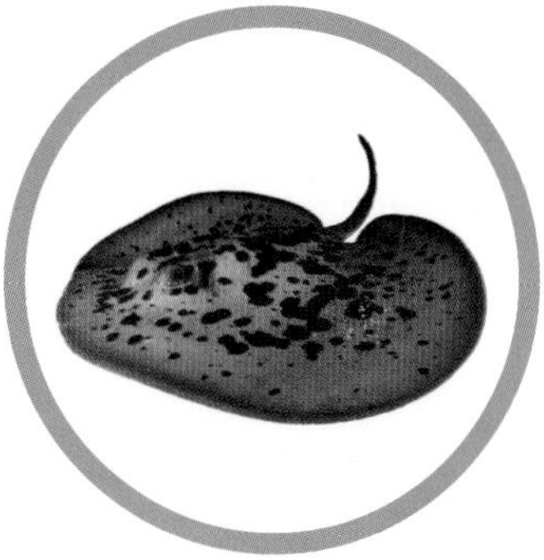
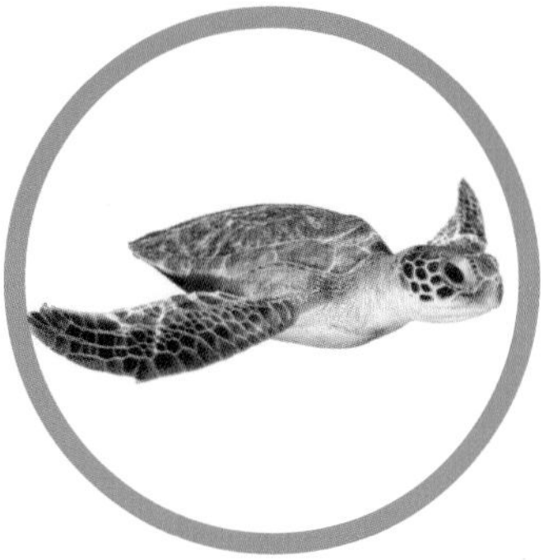
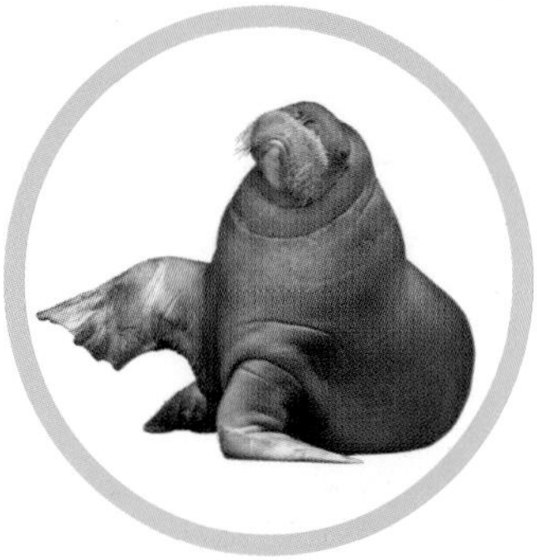

Answers on page 120.

What's Next?

Something is happening to the moon. What will happen next?

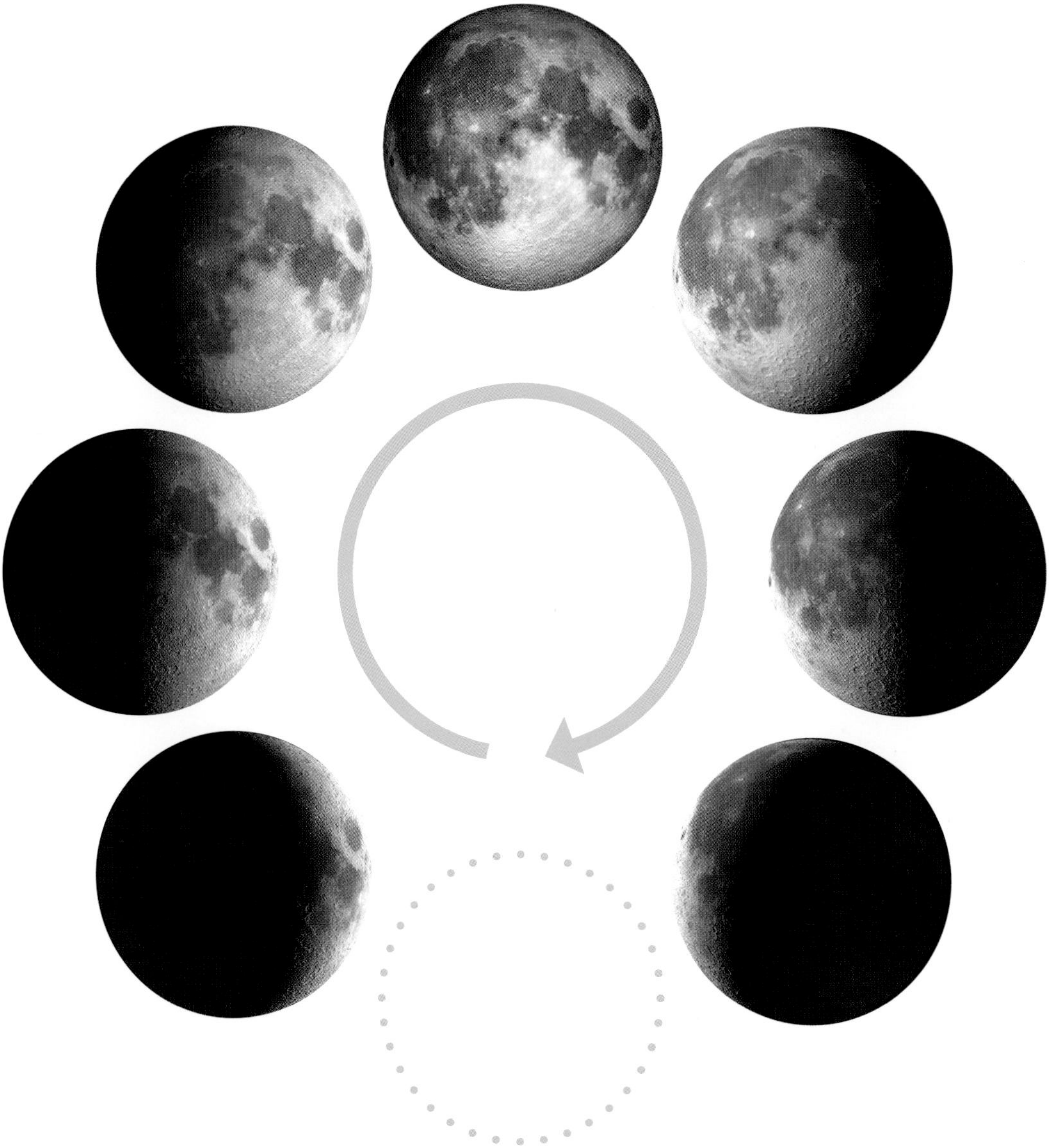

Answers on page 120.

Draw It

The dandelion is missing some parts. Can you draw in the missing flower, stems, and leaves?

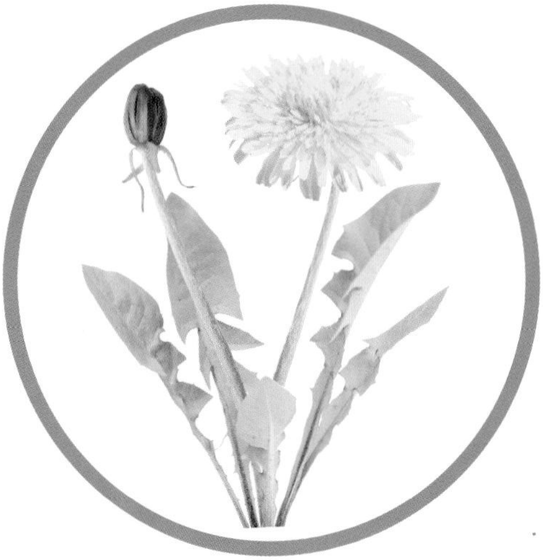

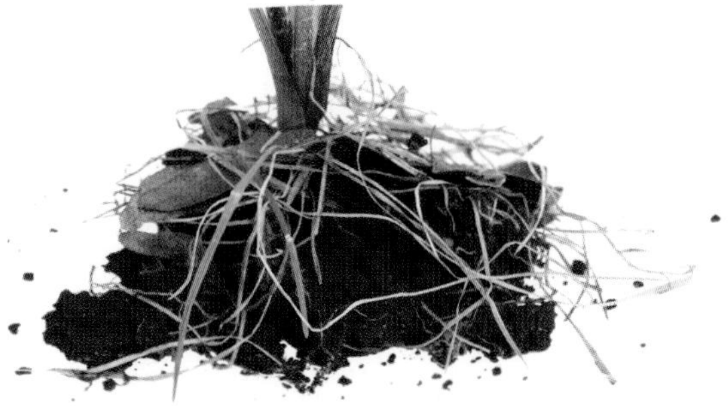

Answers on page 121.

Patterns

Finish each pattern.

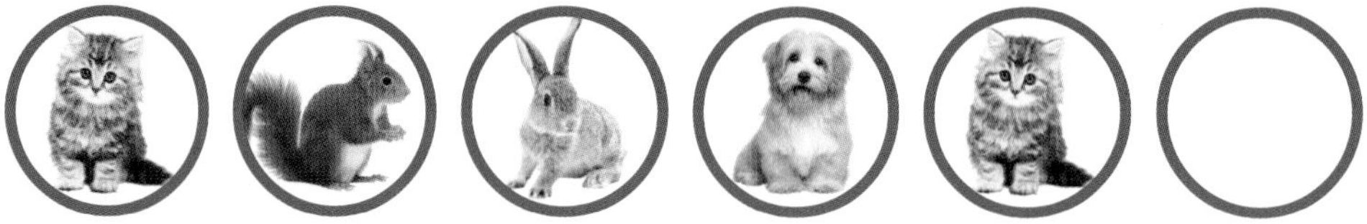

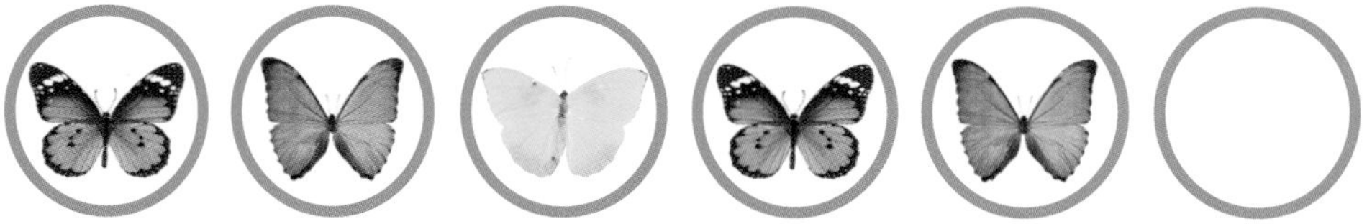

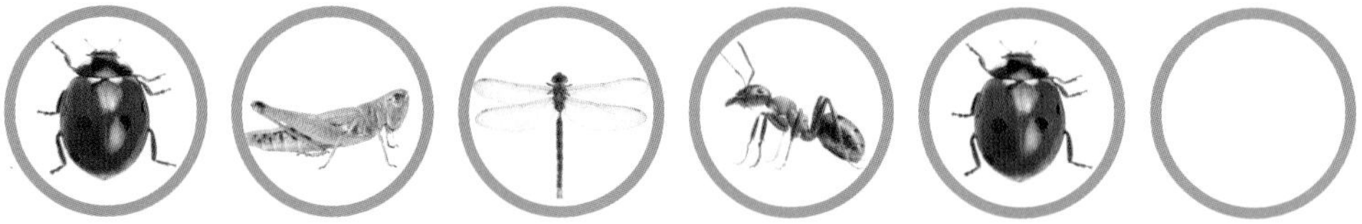

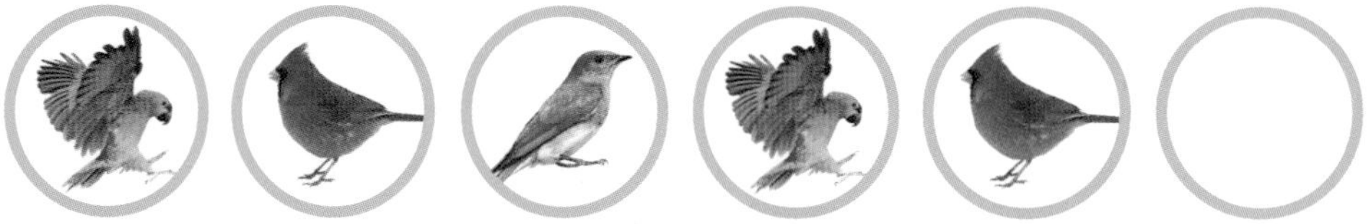

Answers on page 121.

Do It

Turn this book on its side. What do you think will happen? Turn the page to find out.

What happened?

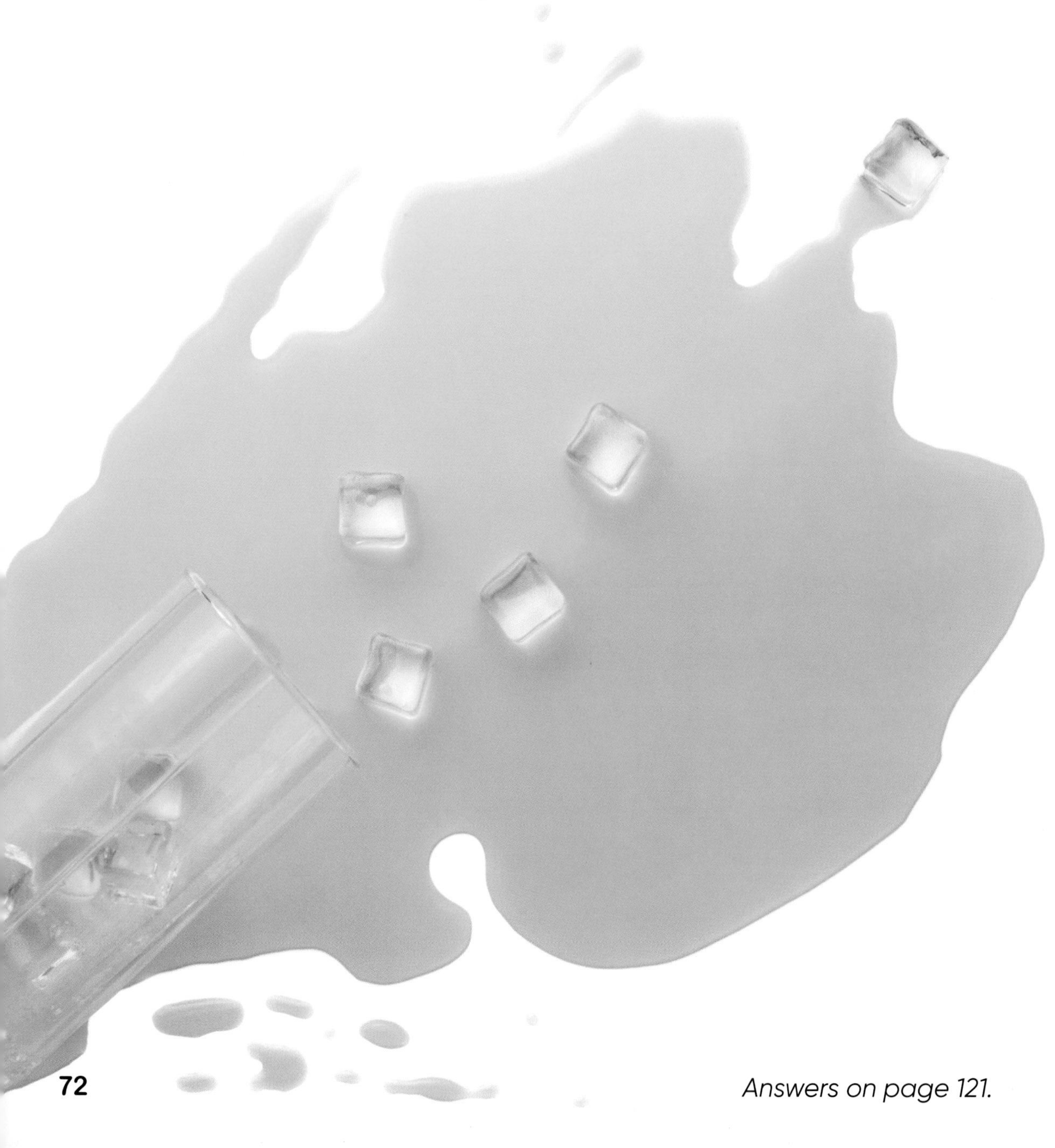

Answers on page 121.

On the Right Path

Follow the path that goes through all the things you need on a rainy day. But avoid the things you need when it's sunny!

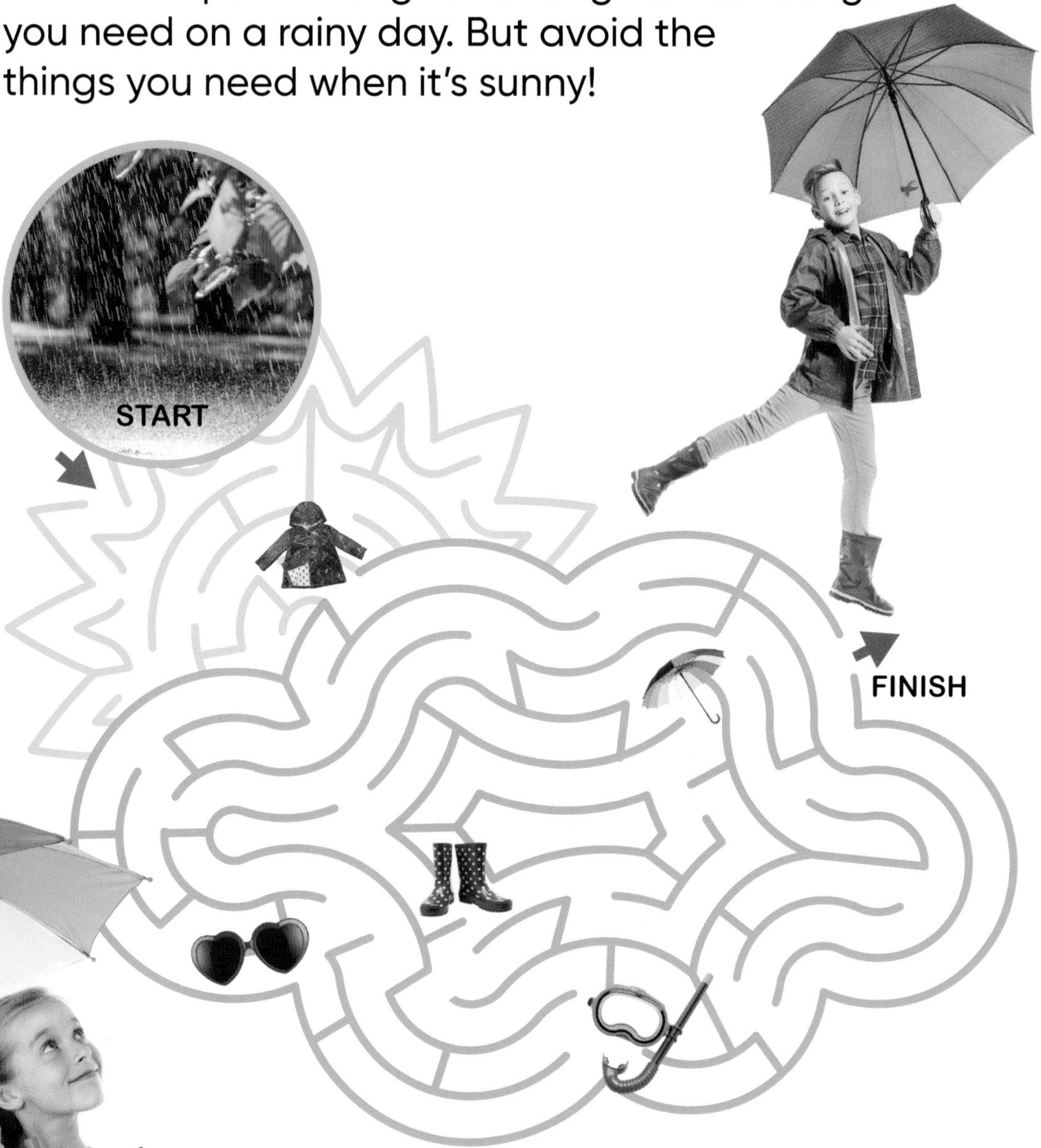
START
FINISH

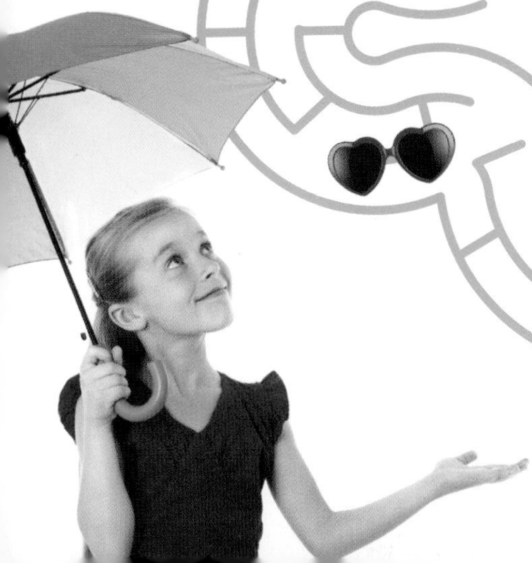

Answers on page 121.

Match It

Draw a line to connect each tool to the first letter of its name.

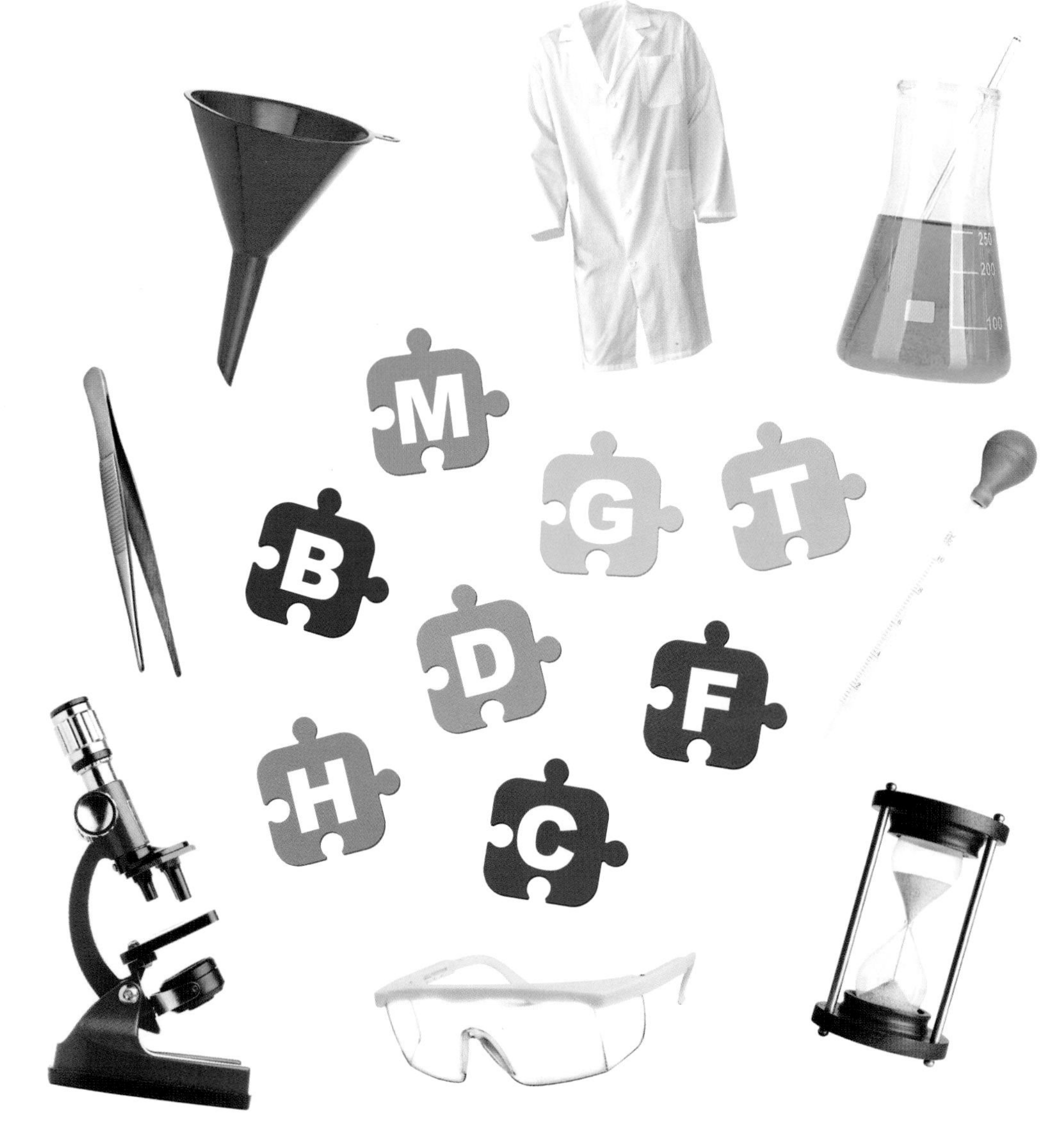
250
200
100
M
G
T
B
D
F
H
C

Answers on page 122.

Shadows

Circle the shadow that matches the robot.

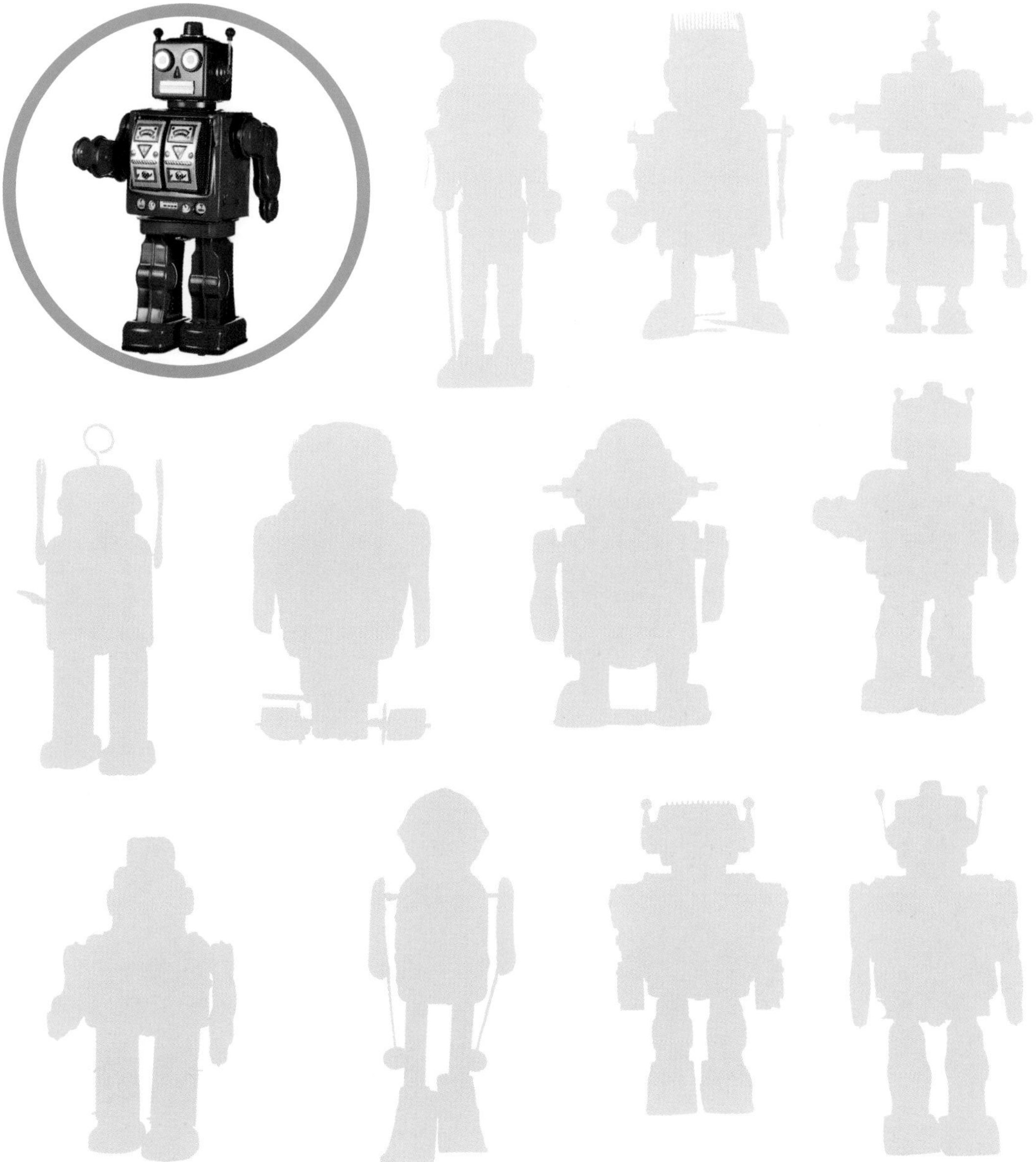

Answers on page 122.

Sink or Float

Changes in water pressure affect how objects float. You can see this in action with condiment packets and a bottle of water. When you squeeze the bottle, the pressure inside is higher. When you let go, the pressure lowers. This makes the packets move.

What you need:

- 4–5 condiment packets of various kinds
- An empty, clear plastic 2-liter bottle with cap (like a soda bottle)
- Water

Directions:

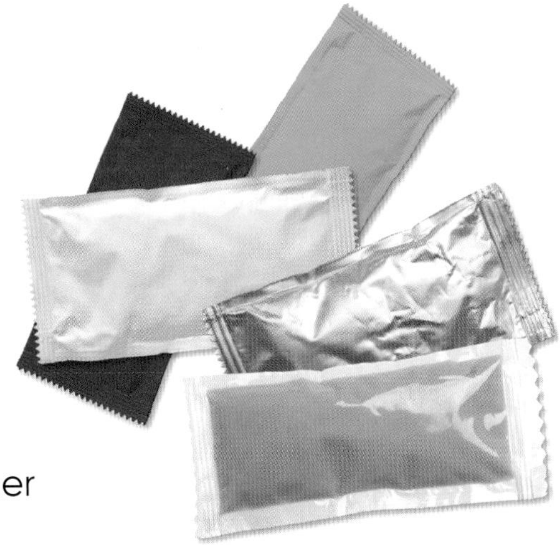

1. Place the condiment packets into the empty bottle.
2. Fill the bottle with water. Screw the cap on the bottle to close it.
3. Look into the bottle. Where are the packets? Are some higher or lower?
4. Gently squeeze the bottle. What do the packets do?
5. Let go of the bottle. What happens inside?

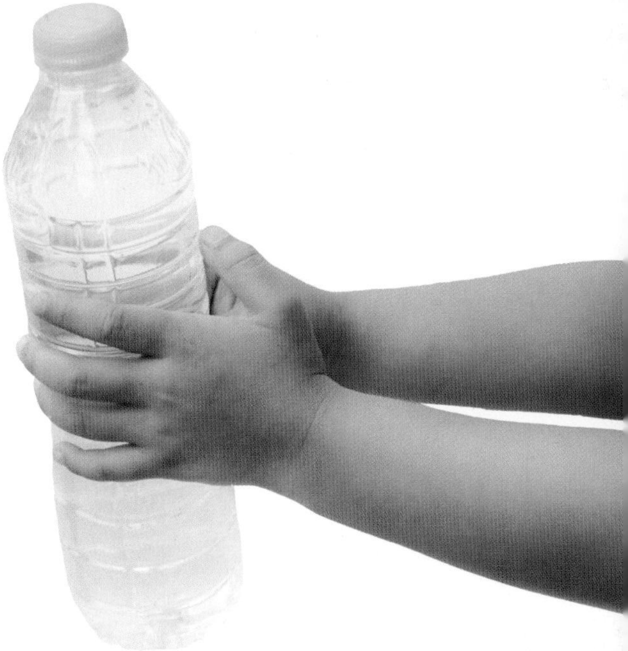

When you squeeze the bottle, what do the packets inside do?

When you let go, what happens to the packets?

Answers on page 122.

What Do I Do?

What am I? What do I help people do?

Answers on page 122.

What Is It?

These objects are all cut up! Can you see what each one is?

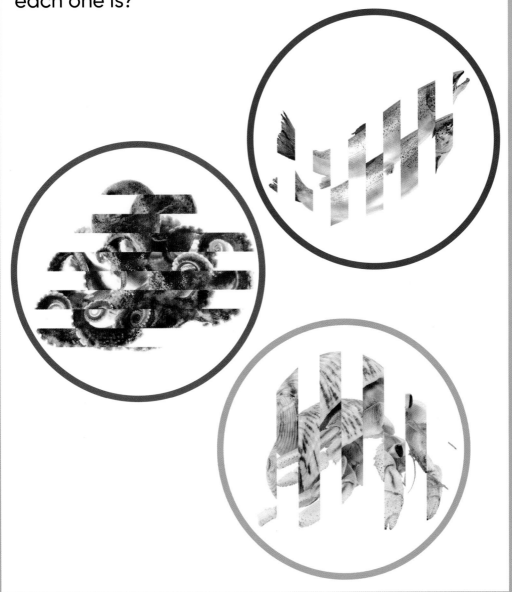

Answers on page 123.

Where Am I?

Point to the parts of the ant.

- ◆ Eye
- ◆ Legs
- ◆ Antennae
- ◆ Pincers

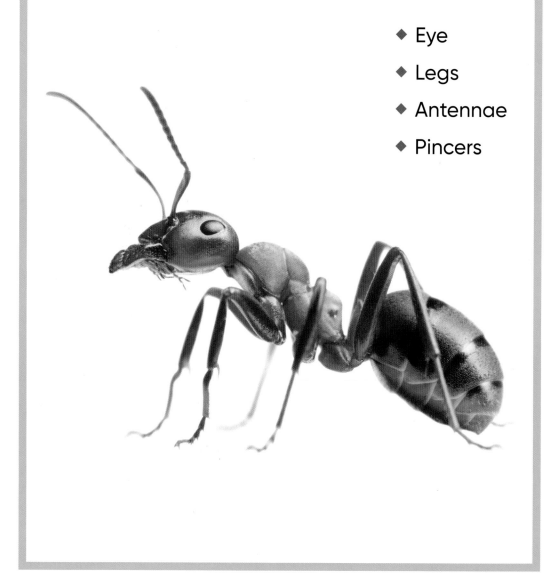

Answers on page 123.

Memory

Look at this picture for 1 minute. Remember as much as you can! Then turn the page.

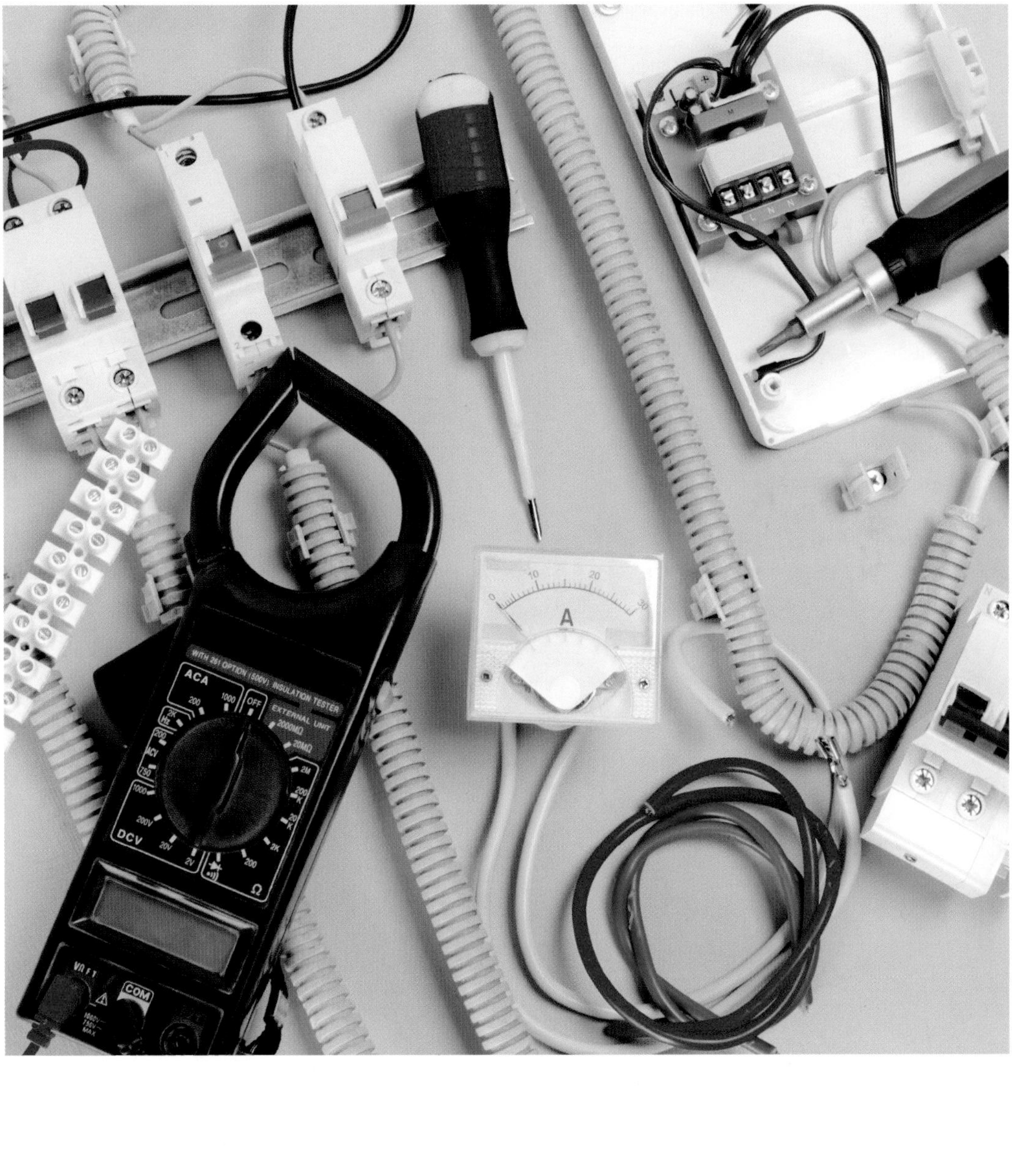
ACA
OFF
DCV
COM
A

What is different in this picture? Find 4 things that are different.

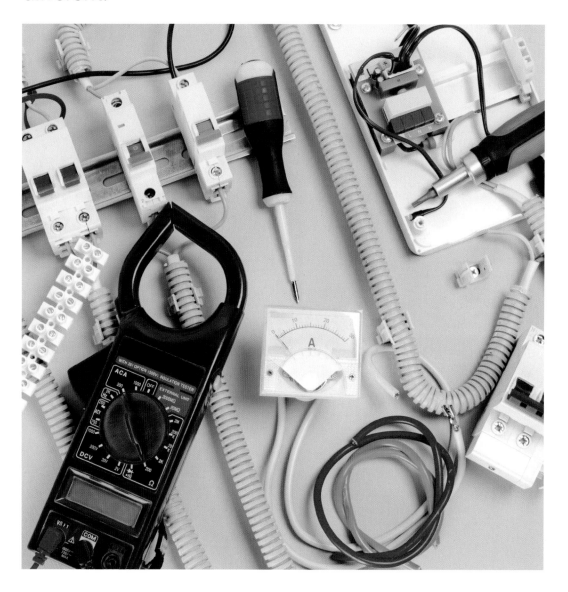

Answers on page 123.

Out of Order

These pictures are in the wrong order! What is the right order?

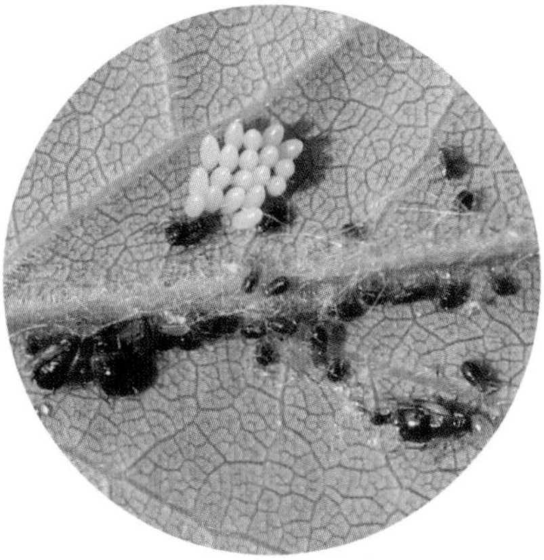

1

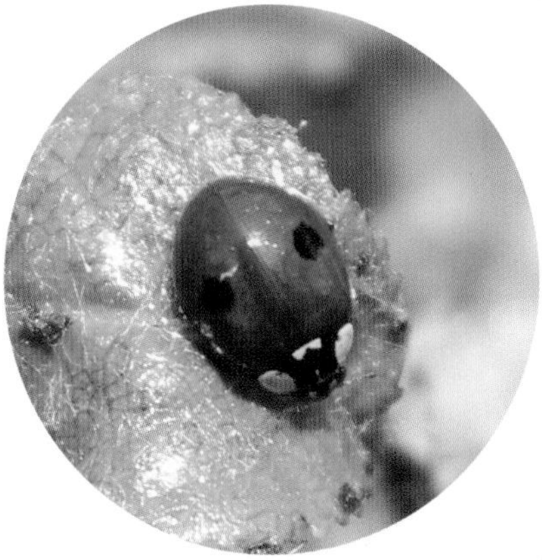

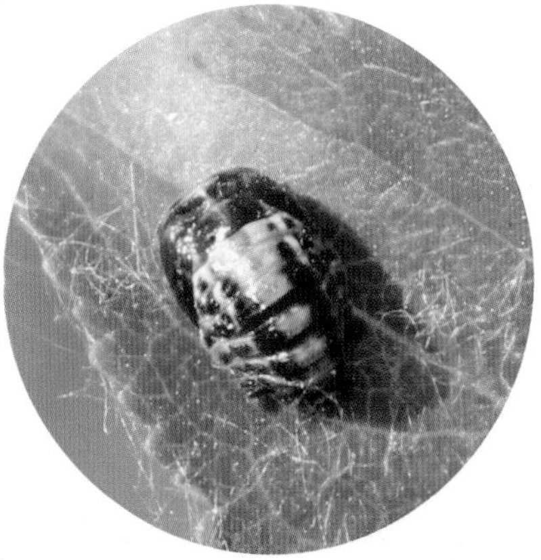

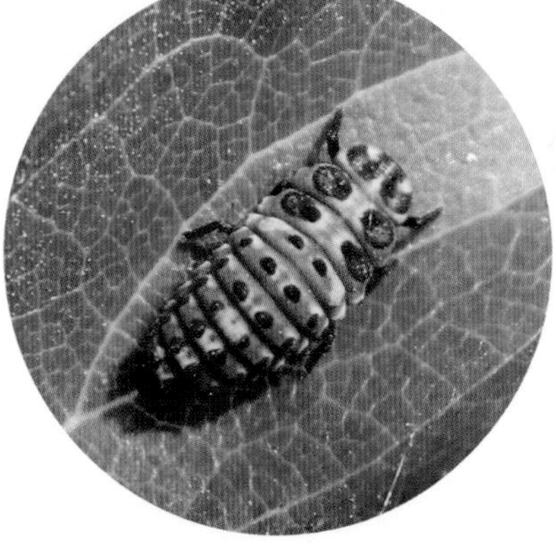

Answers on page 123.

Missing Piece

Circle the piece that goes in the missing spot.

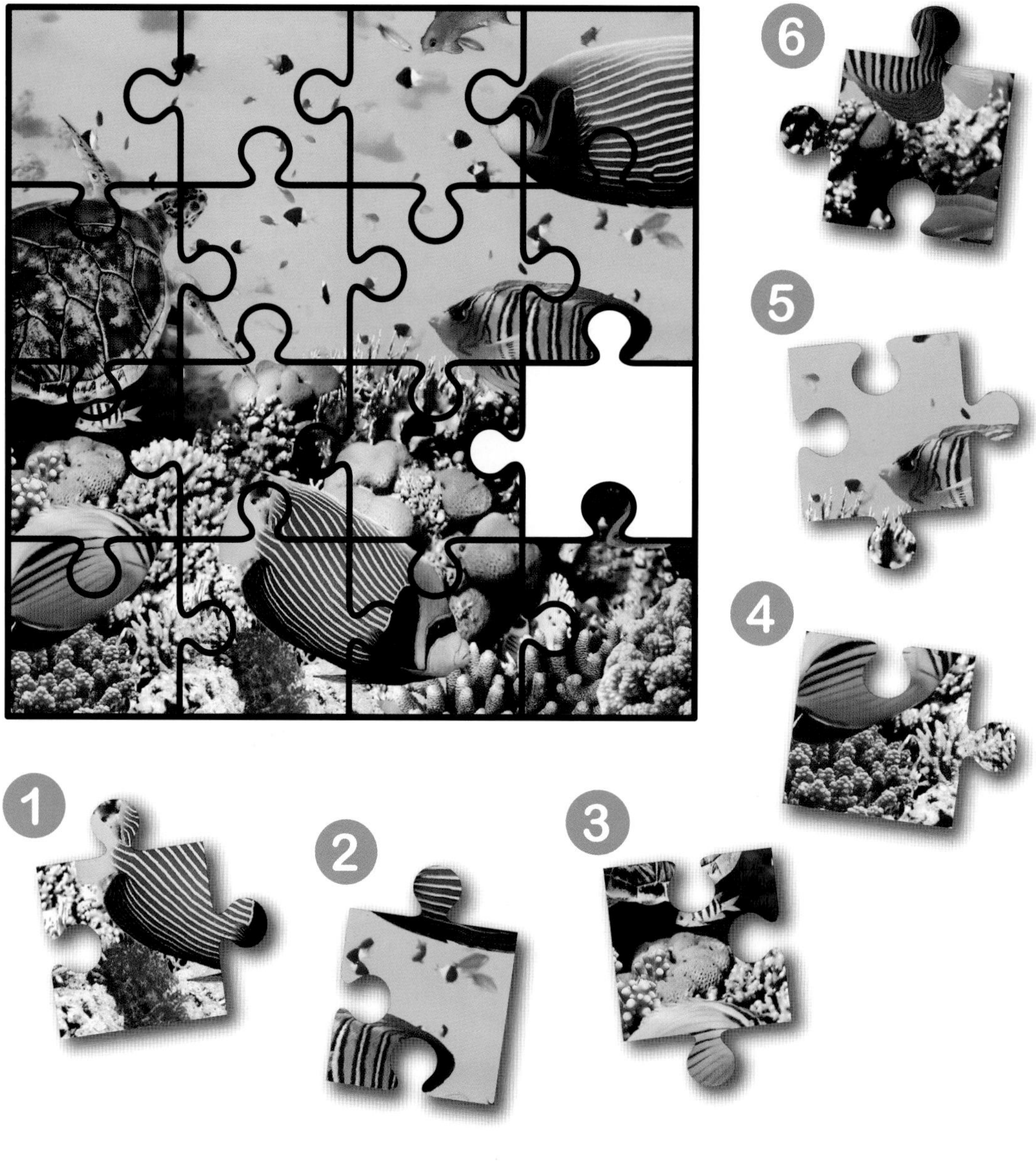
6
5
4
1
2
3

Answers on page 124.

Zoom In

Draw a line from each zoomed picture to the object it matches.

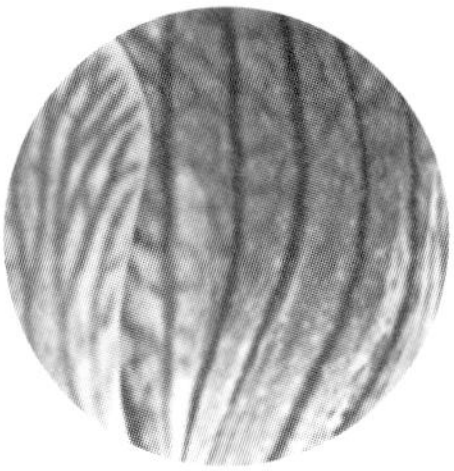
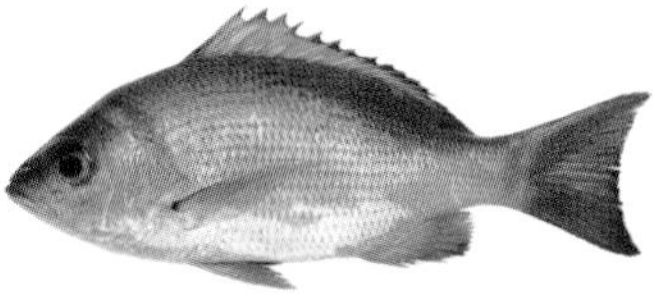

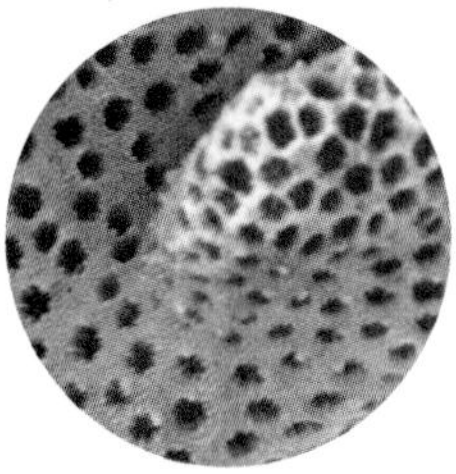
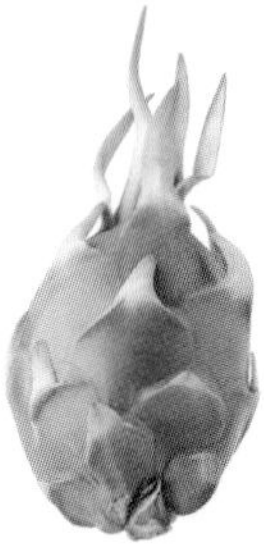

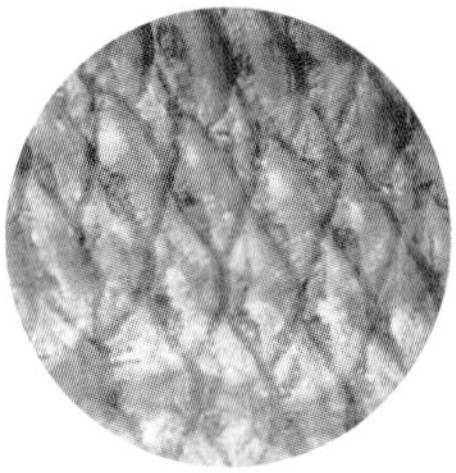
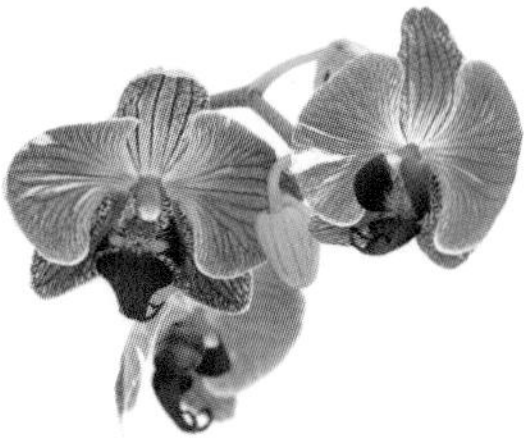

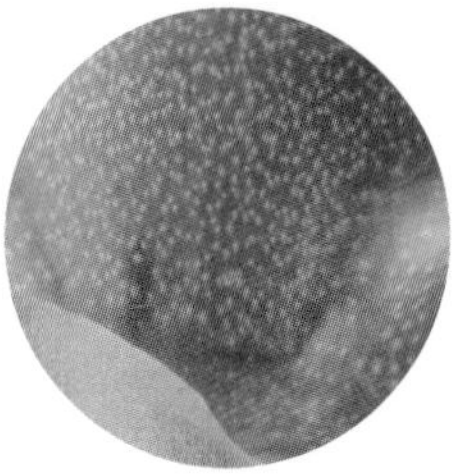
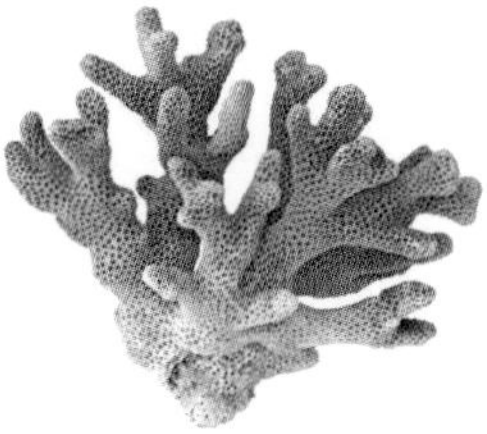

Answers on page 124.

Something's Wrong

What's wrong in this picture? Find 6 mistakes.

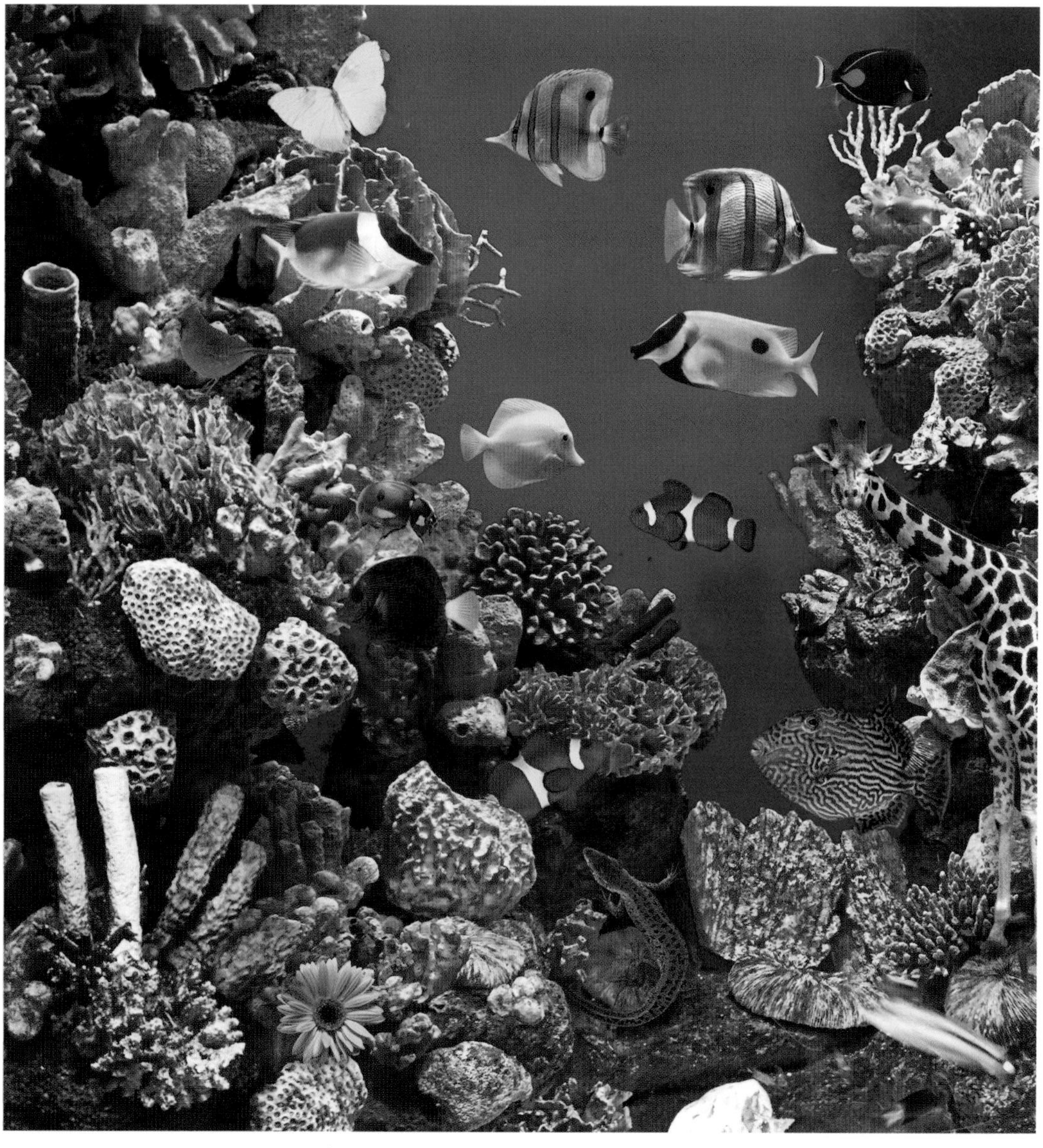

Answers on page 124.

Clues

I saw a cool bug today. Use the clues to figure out which bug I saw!

The bug has 6 legs.

The bug can fly.

The bug does not sting.

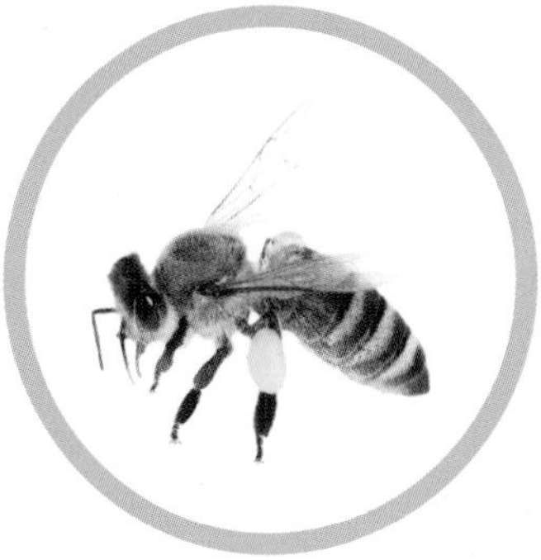
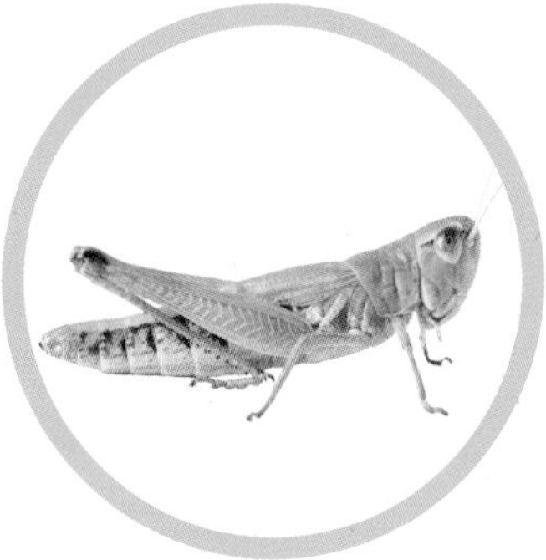
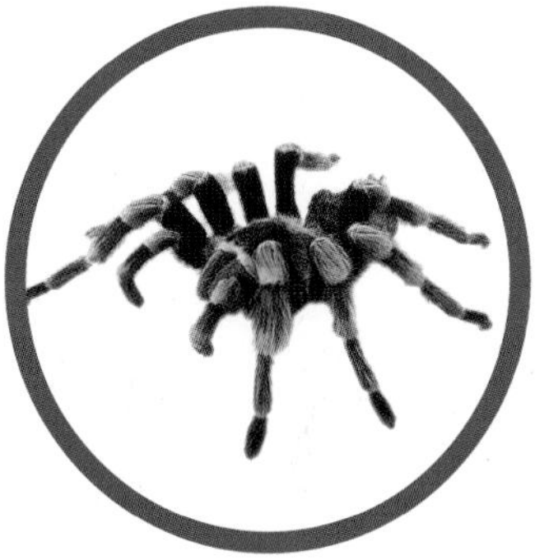
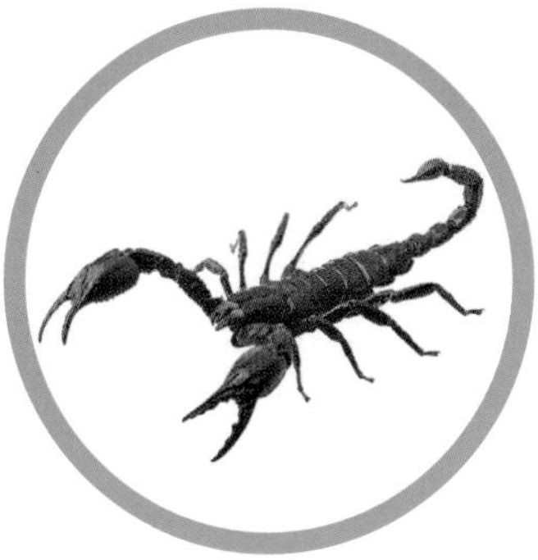
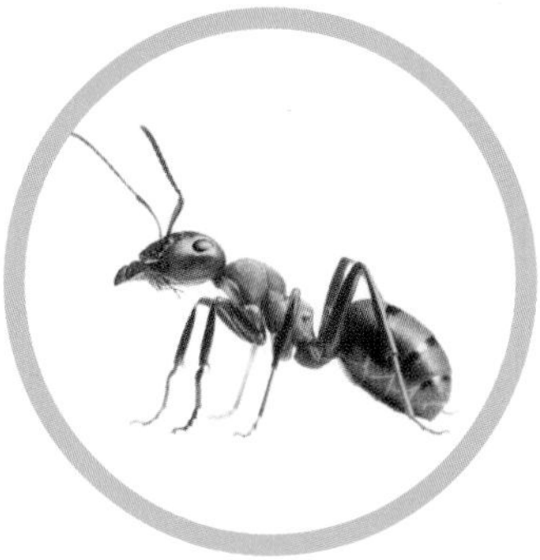
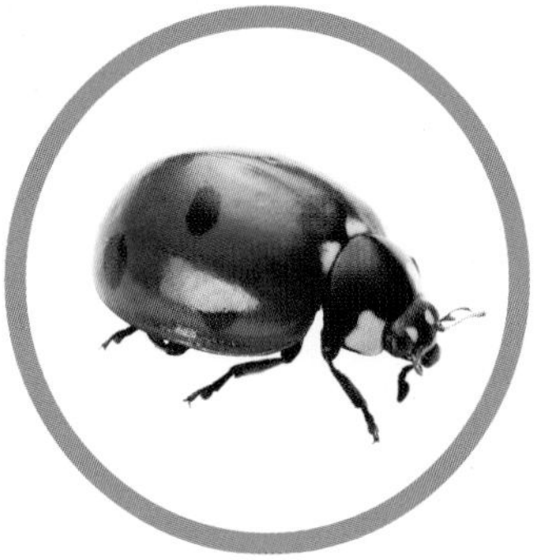

Answers on page 124.

Groups

Write the number of objects that fit in each group.
Some might fit in more than one group!

Are red? _____

Are used to build? _____

Help you see in the dark? _____

Have buttons? _____

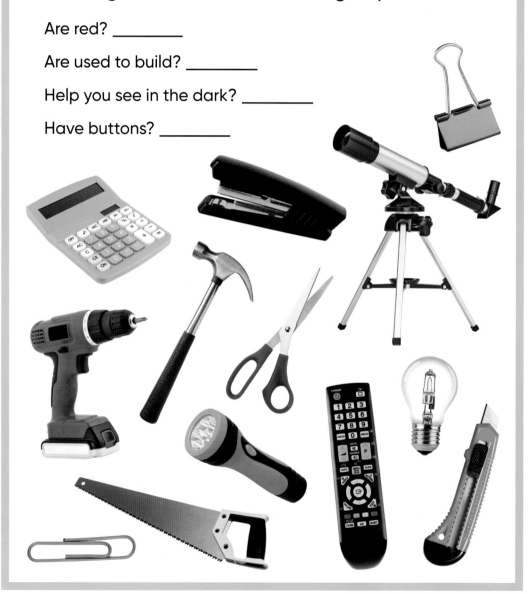

Answers on page 125.

Which Ones?

Circle all of the vegetables that grow underground.

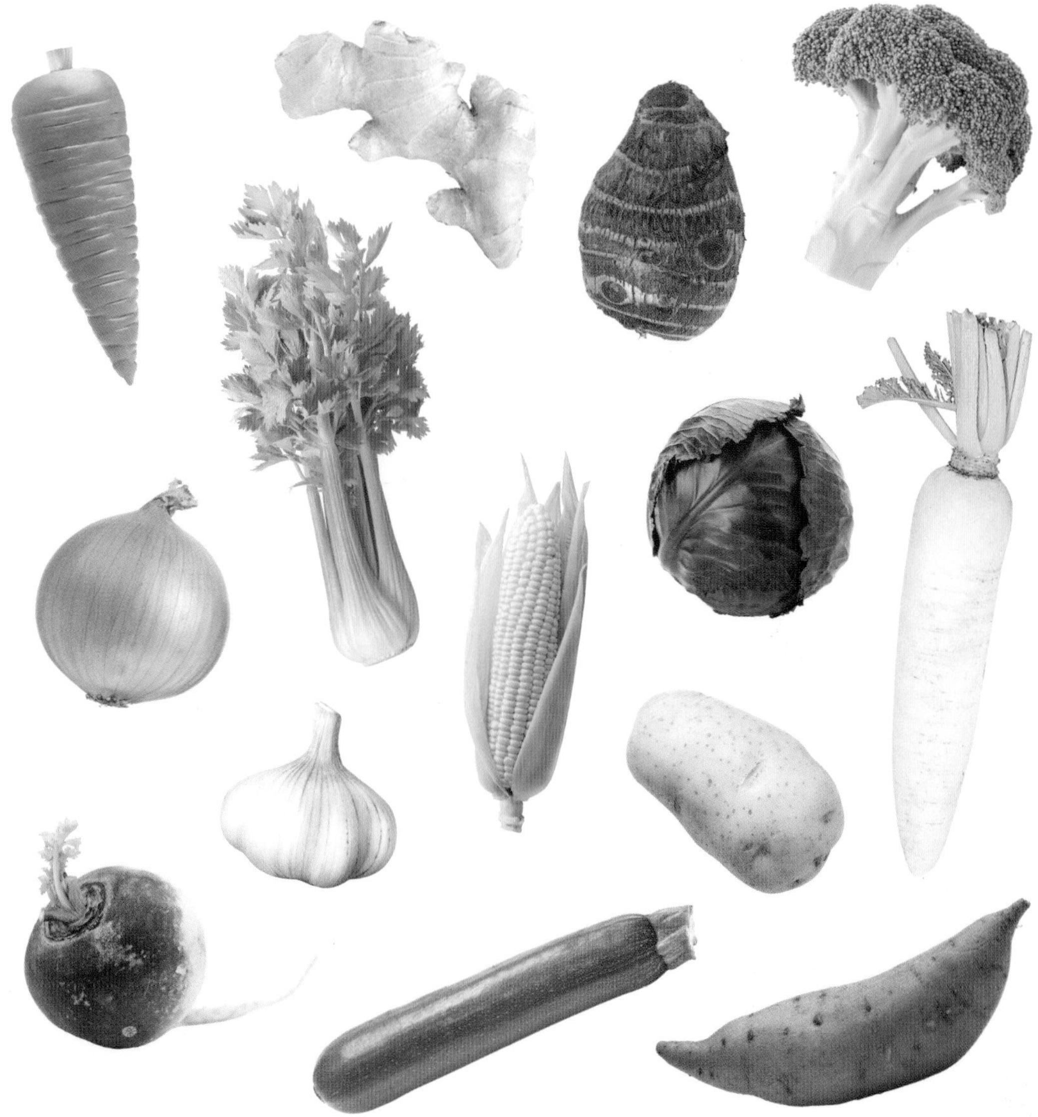

Answers on page 125.

What's Different?

Circle the 7 differences between these pictures.

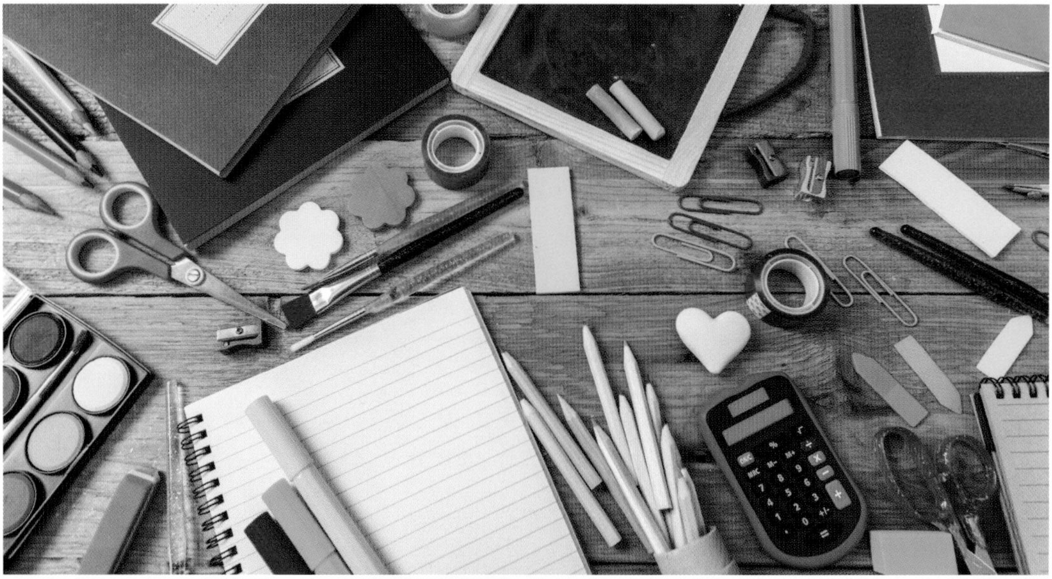
%
M+
M-
MC
7
8
9
4
5
6
1
2
3
0
+/-
=
+
-
×

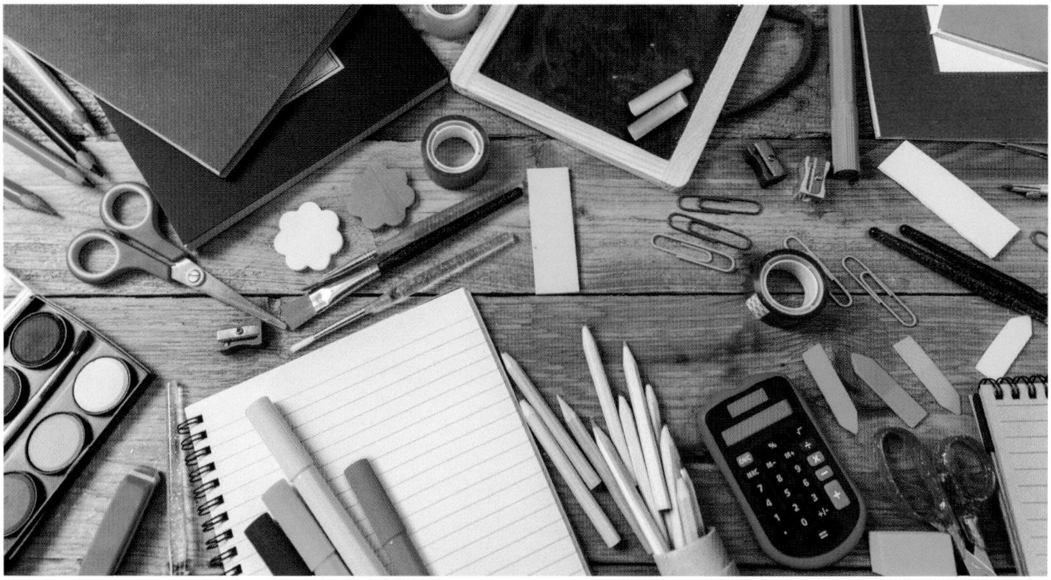

Answers on page 125.

Patterns

Fill in the missing piece of each pattern.

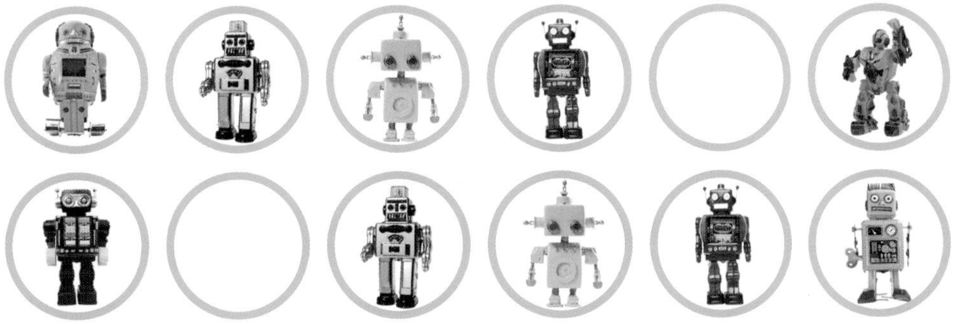

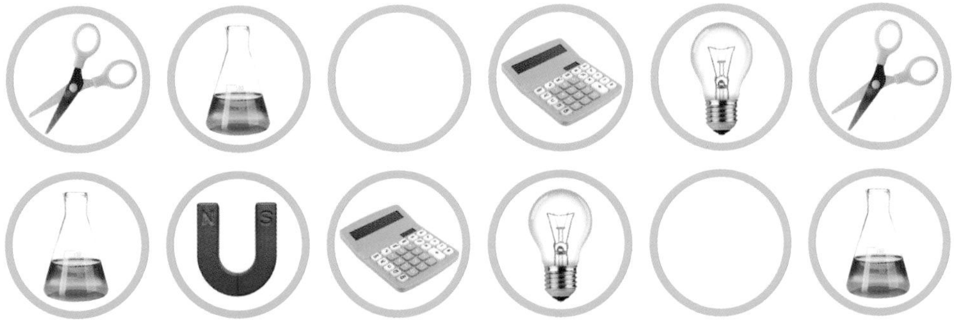

N
S

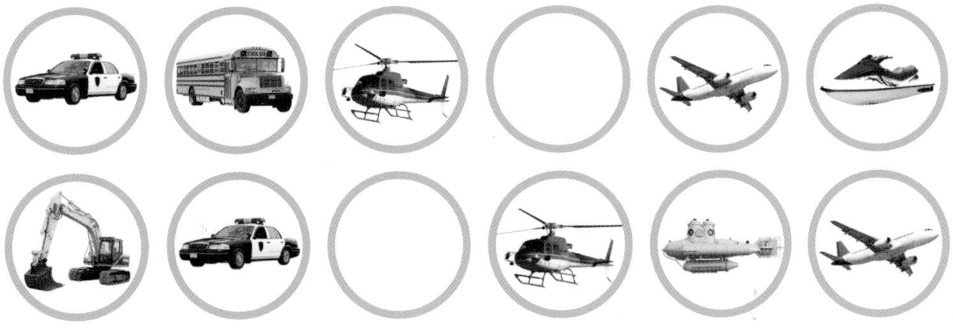

Answers on page 125.

Hide and Seek

Find the animals and shell hiding in the ocean.

1 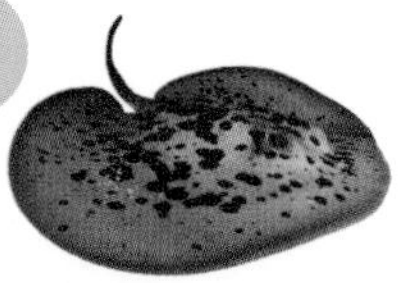 2 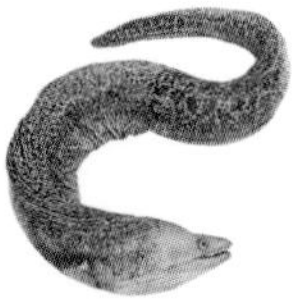 3 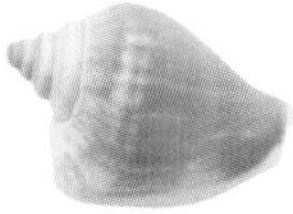 4 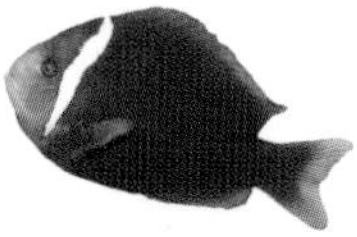

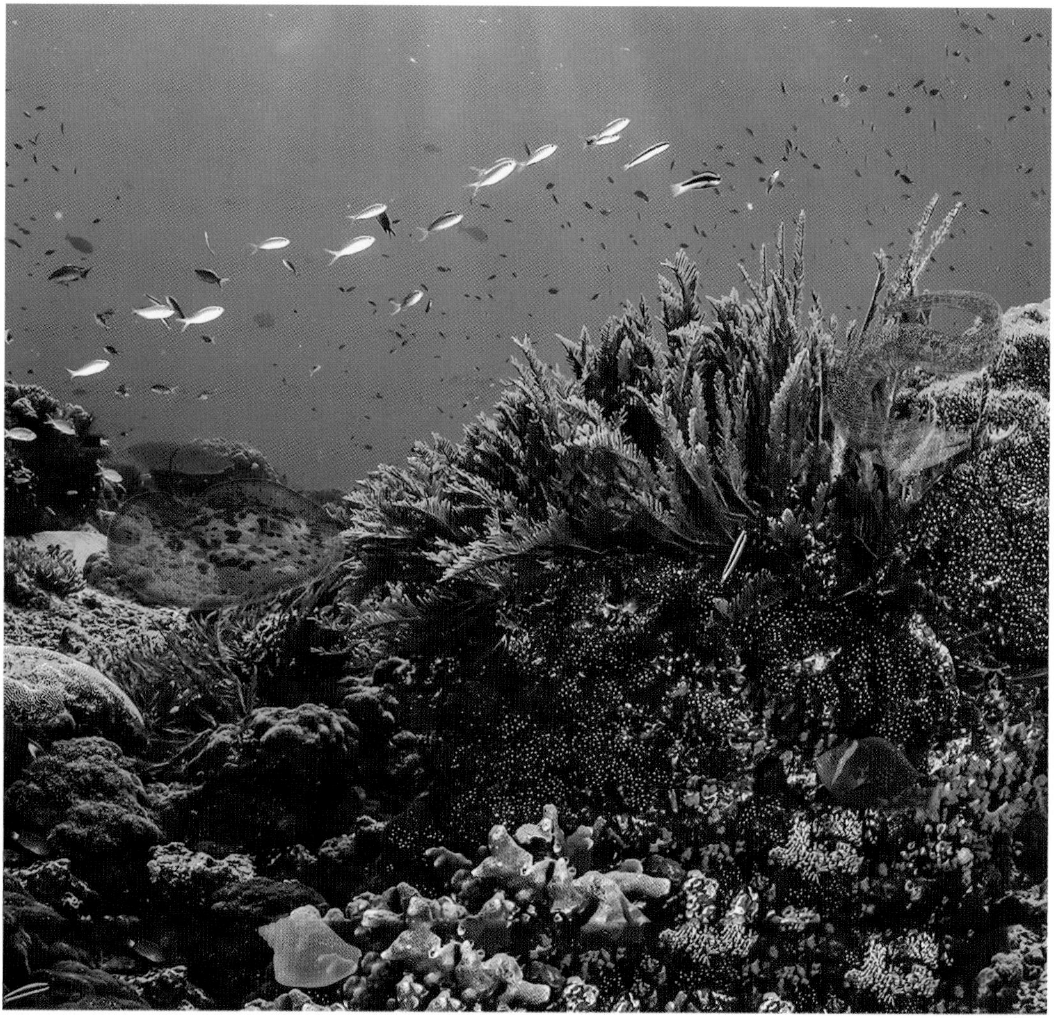

Answers on page 126.

Draw It

The dinosaur skeleton is missing some parts! Can you draw in its missing body?

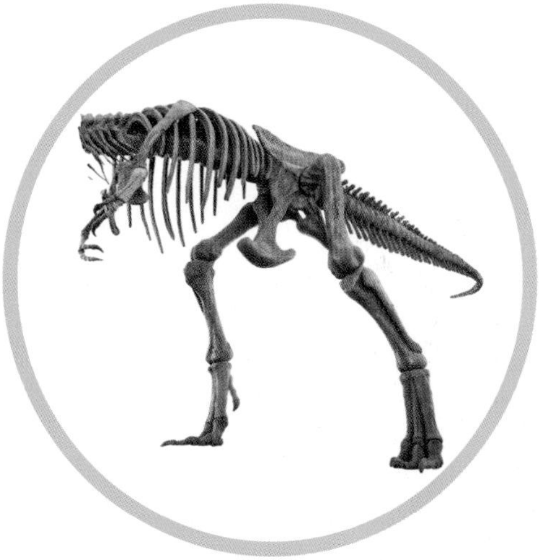

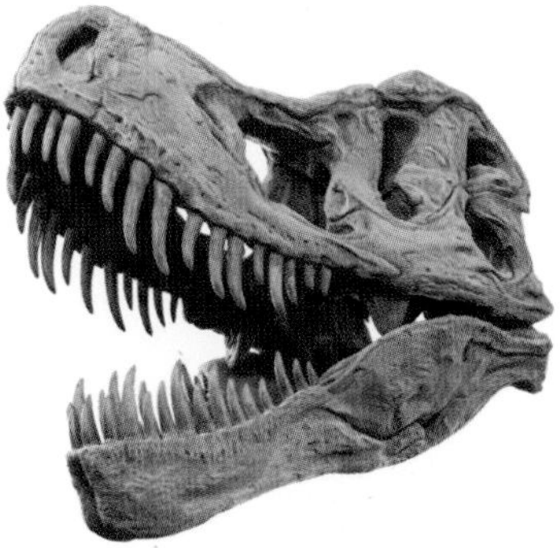

Answers on page 126.

On the Right Path

Follow the path that goes through every robot part. But avoid the flowers!

START

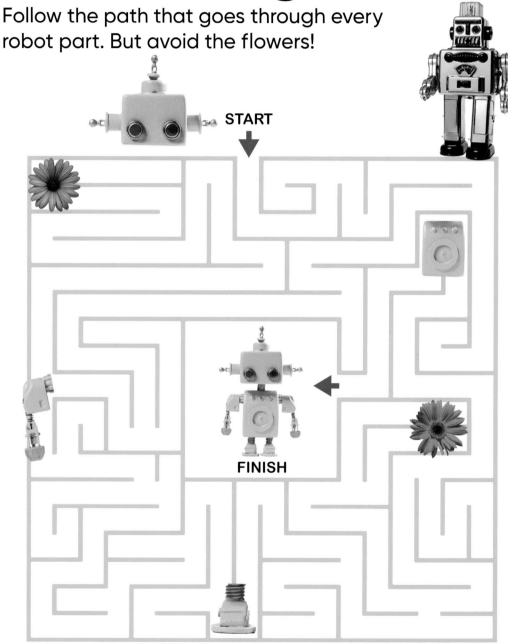

FINISH

94

Answers on page 126.

Patterns

Fill in the missing piece of each pattern.

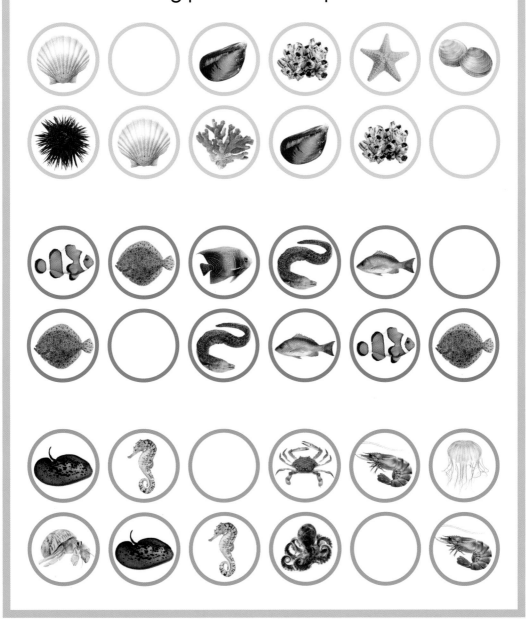

Where Am I?

How well can you tell where all your limbs are? What about when your eyes are closed? You might be surprised how hard it is when you can't see.

What you need:

- A friend

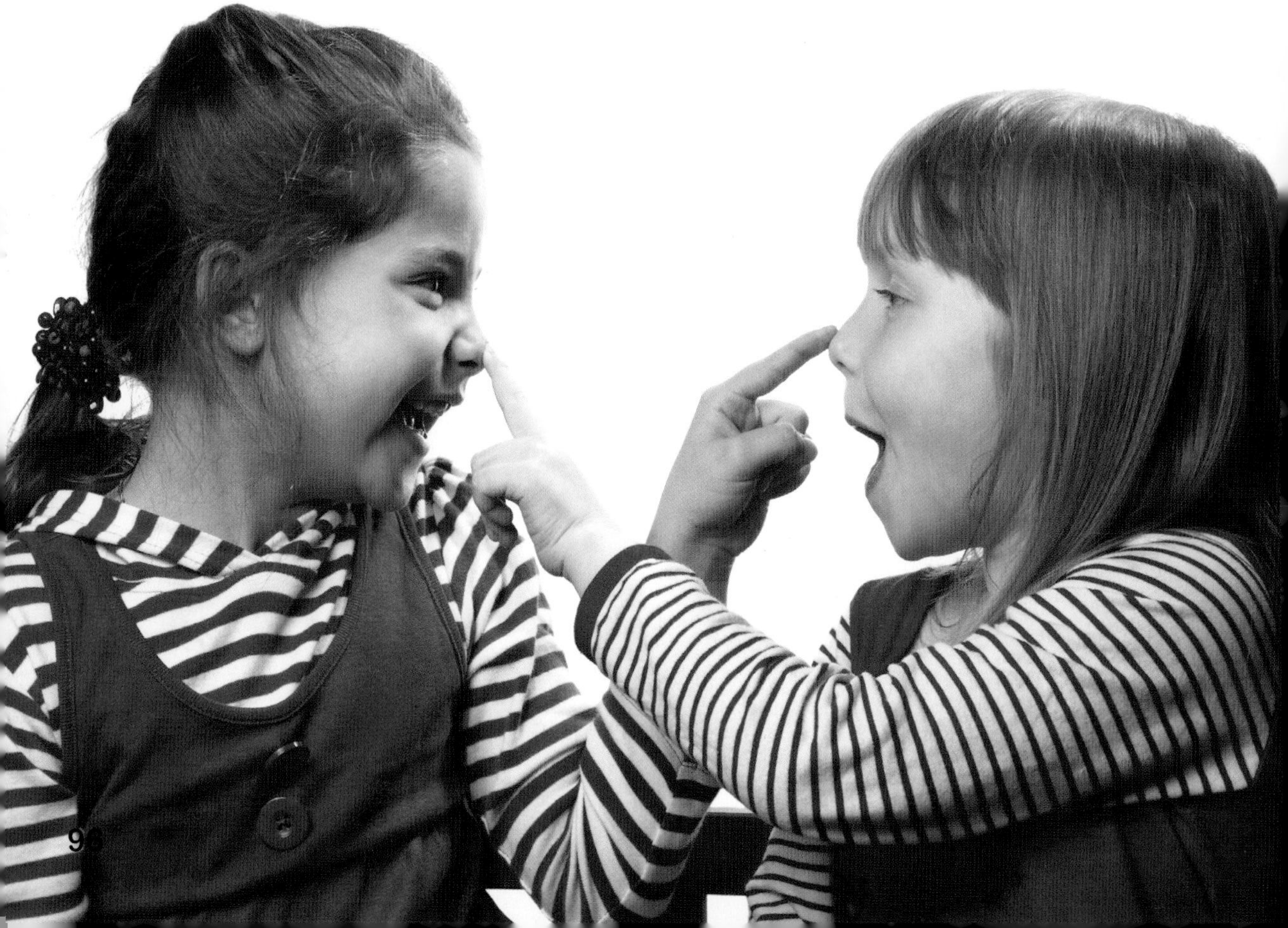

Activity 1:

1. Hold your left hand up about 6 inches in front of your face.
2. With one finger on your right hand, touch your nose then a finger on your left hand, then your nose again. Go back and forth as quickly as you can.
3. Now close your eyes and do the same thing. Your friend will say how far you are from your target if you miss.
4. Switch hands and try again.

How fast are you able to go with your eyes open? How does that compare to when your eyes are closed?

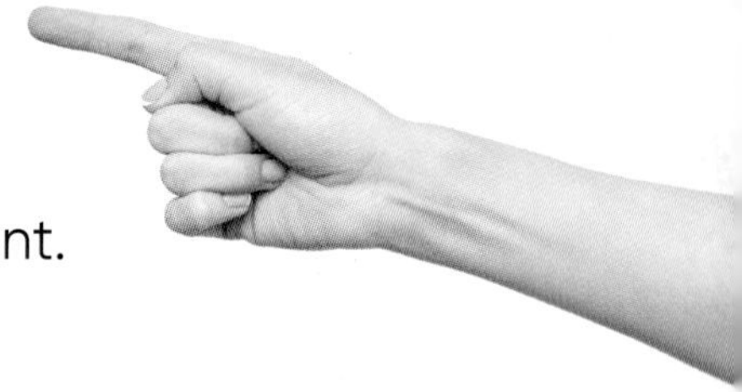

Activity 2:

1. Hold your hand out, your arm just a little bent.
2. Touch your thumb with your other hand.
3. Have your friend move your hand to a new position. Touch your thumb again.
4. Try this again in 3 more positions.
5. Now close your eyes and try the same thing. Your friend will say how far you are from your target if you miss.
6. Switch hands and try again.

How many times are you able to find your thumb with your eyes open? What about with closed eyes?

Answers on page 127.

Shadows

Circle the shadow that matches the dinosaur.

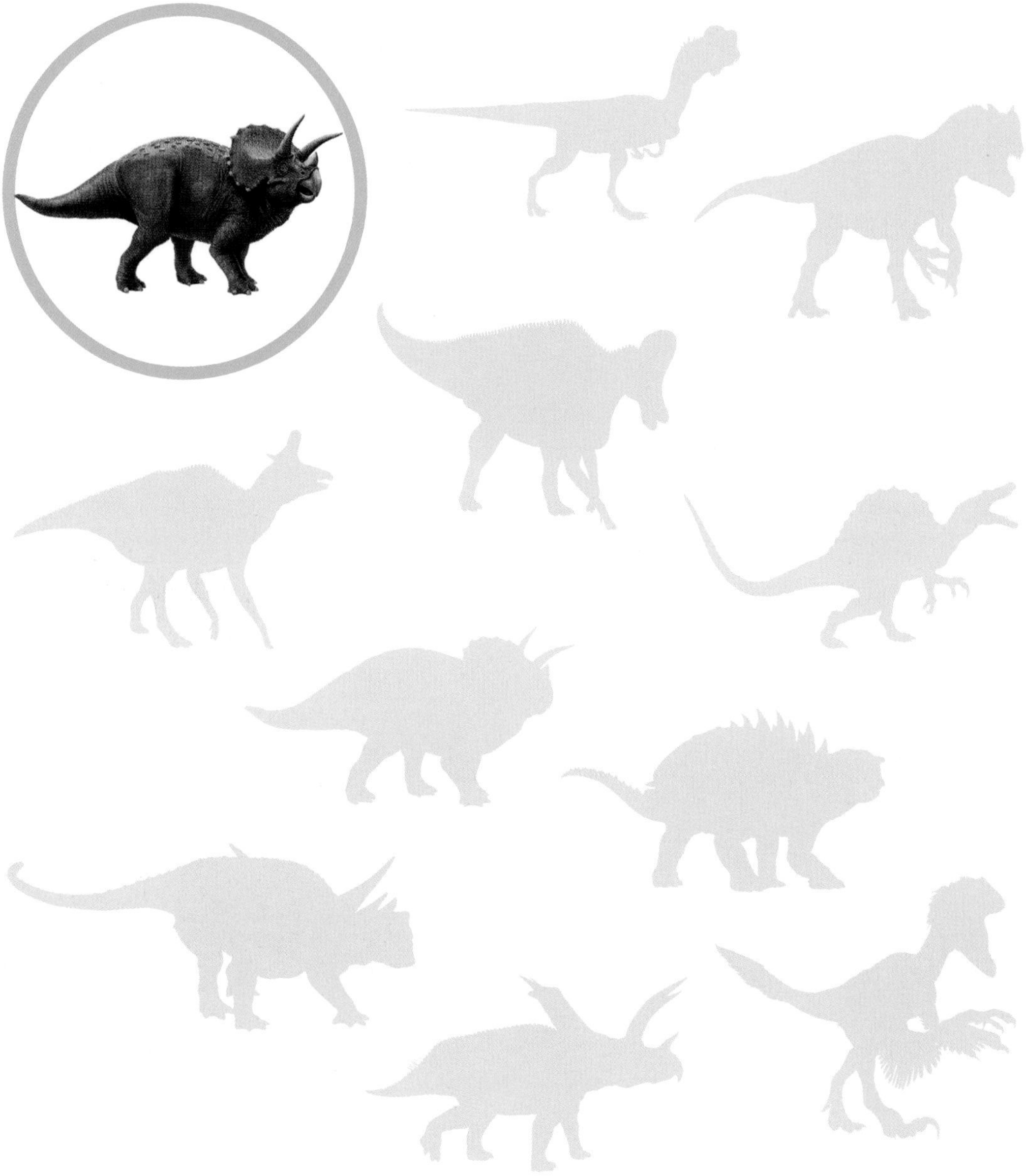

Answers on page 127.

Clues

I lost my measuring tool! Use the clues to figure out which tool is mine.

My tool is not blue.

My tool has hands.

My tool is not electronic

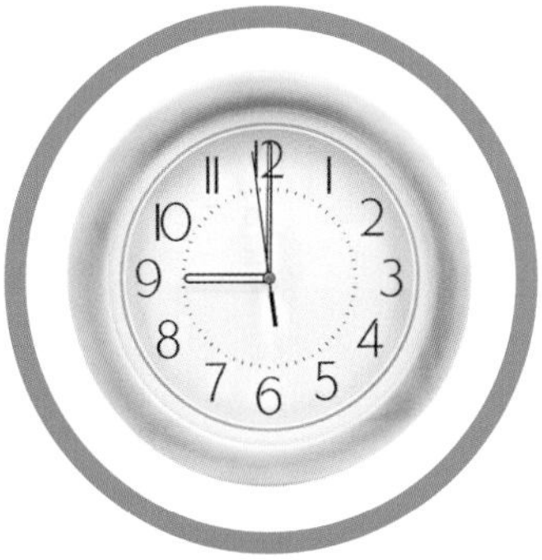
12
1
2
3
4
5
6
7
8
9
10
11

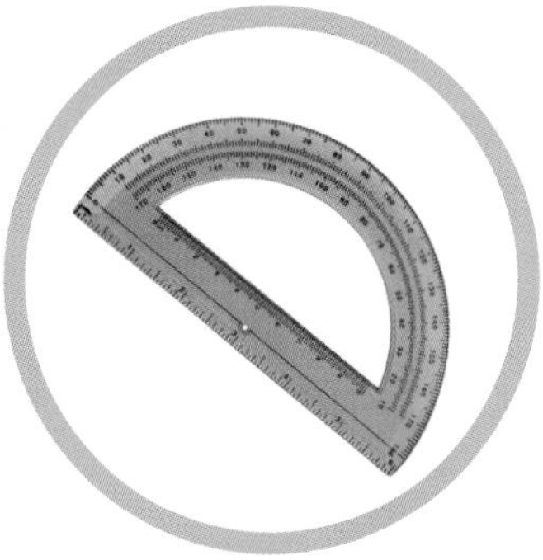

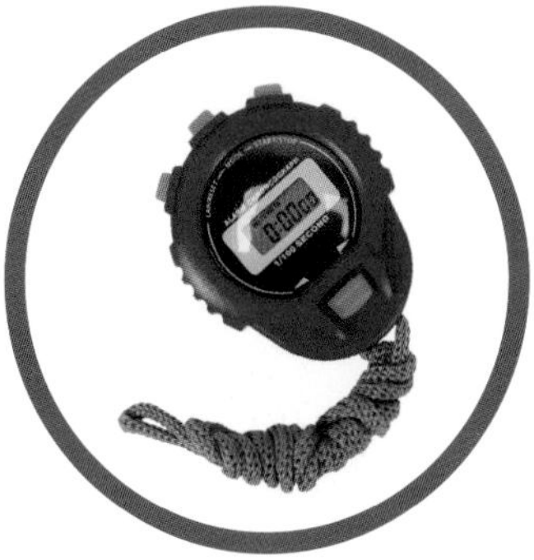

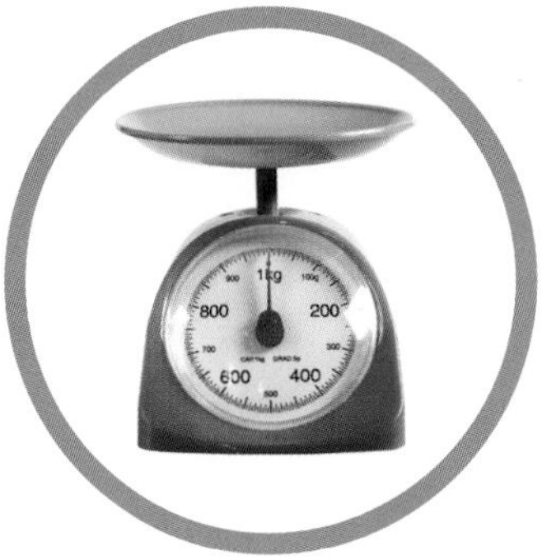
1kg
800
200
600
400

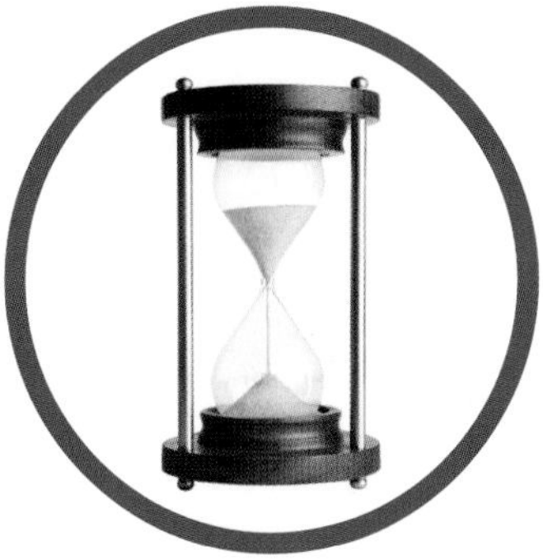

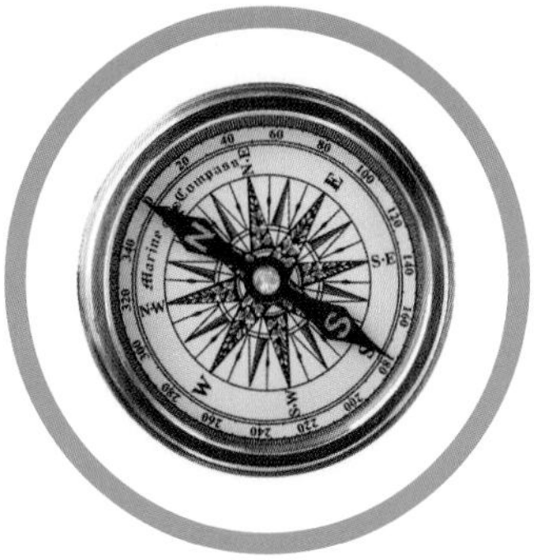

Answers on page 127.

Where Am I?

Point to each object in space.

◆ Earth   ◆ Saturn   ◆ Mercury

◆ Sun   ◆ Mars   ◆ Uranus

◆ Jupiter   ◆ Neptune   ◆ Venus

Answers on page 127.

Out of Order

These pictures are in the wrong order! What is the right order?

Answers on page 128.

What Is It?

These objects are all cut up! Can you see what each one is?

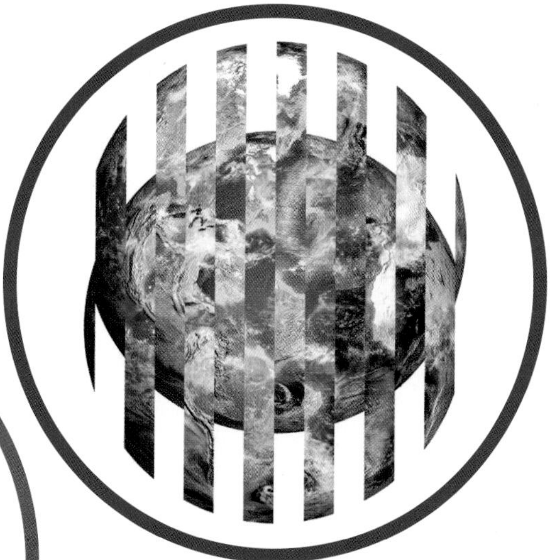

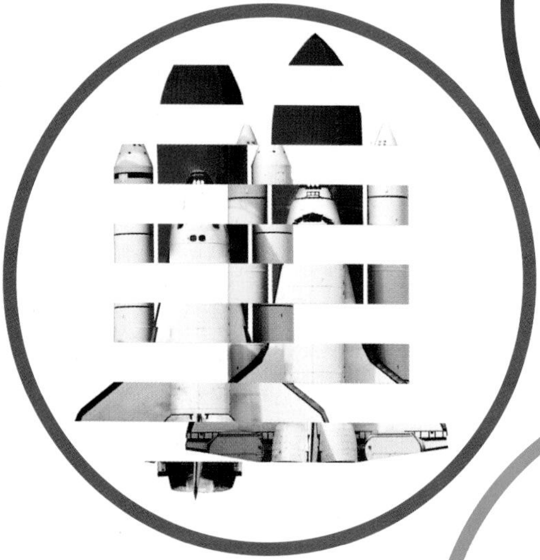

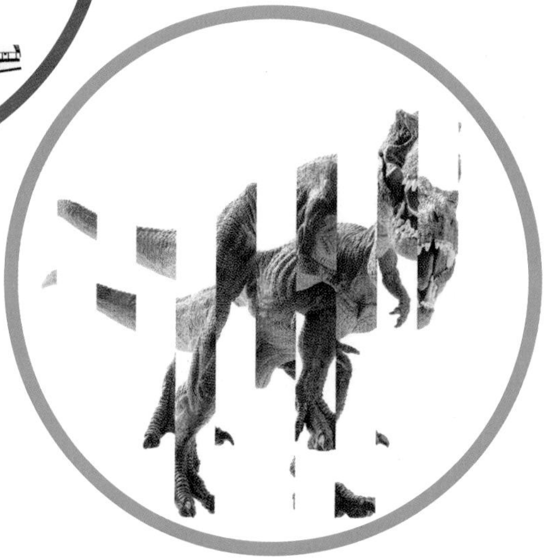

Answers on page 128.

Do It

Poke the picture. What do you think will happen? Turn the page to find out.

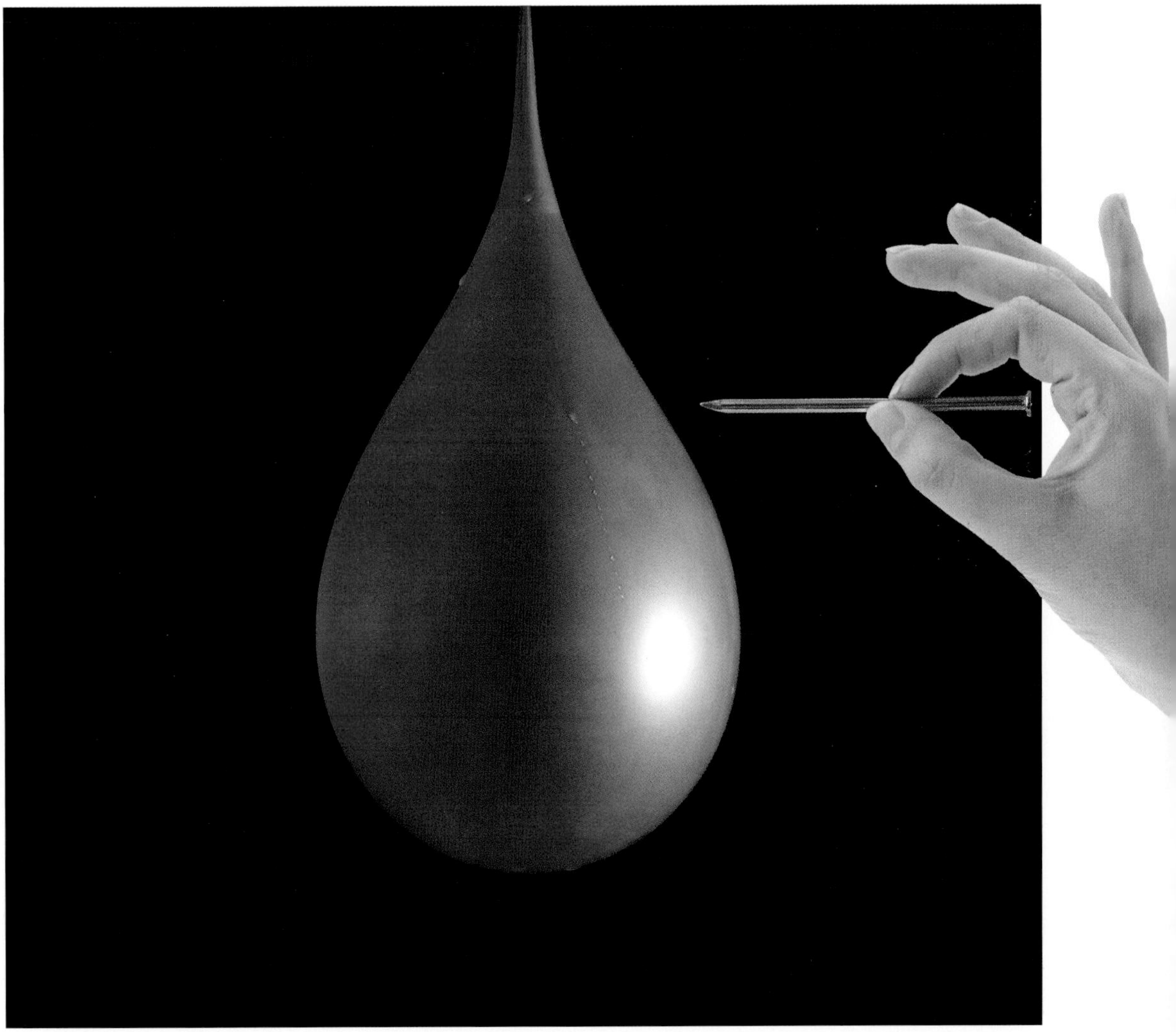

What happened?

Answers on page 128.

Memory

Look at this picture for 1 minute. Remember as much as you can! Then turn the page.

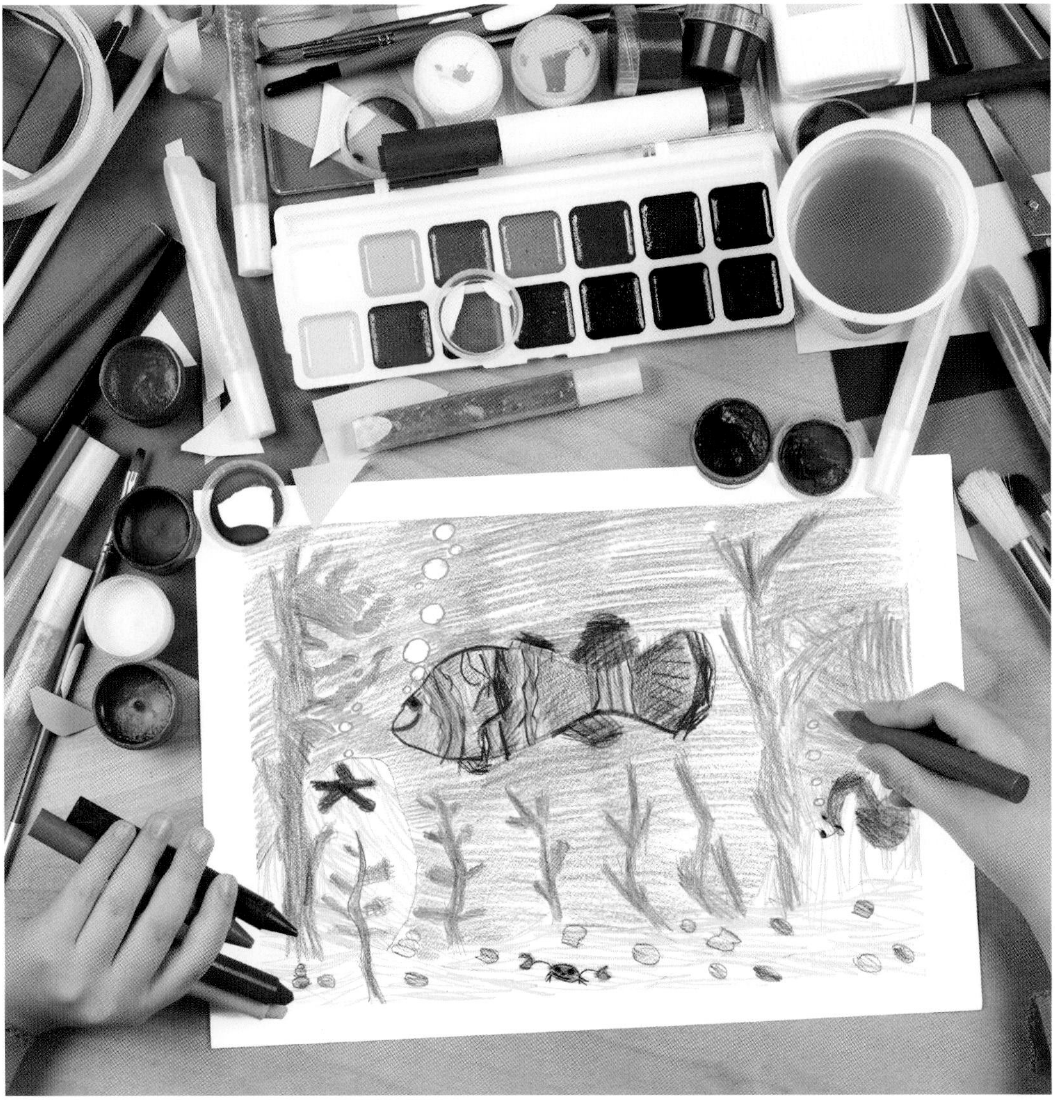

What is different in this picture? Find 5 things that are different.

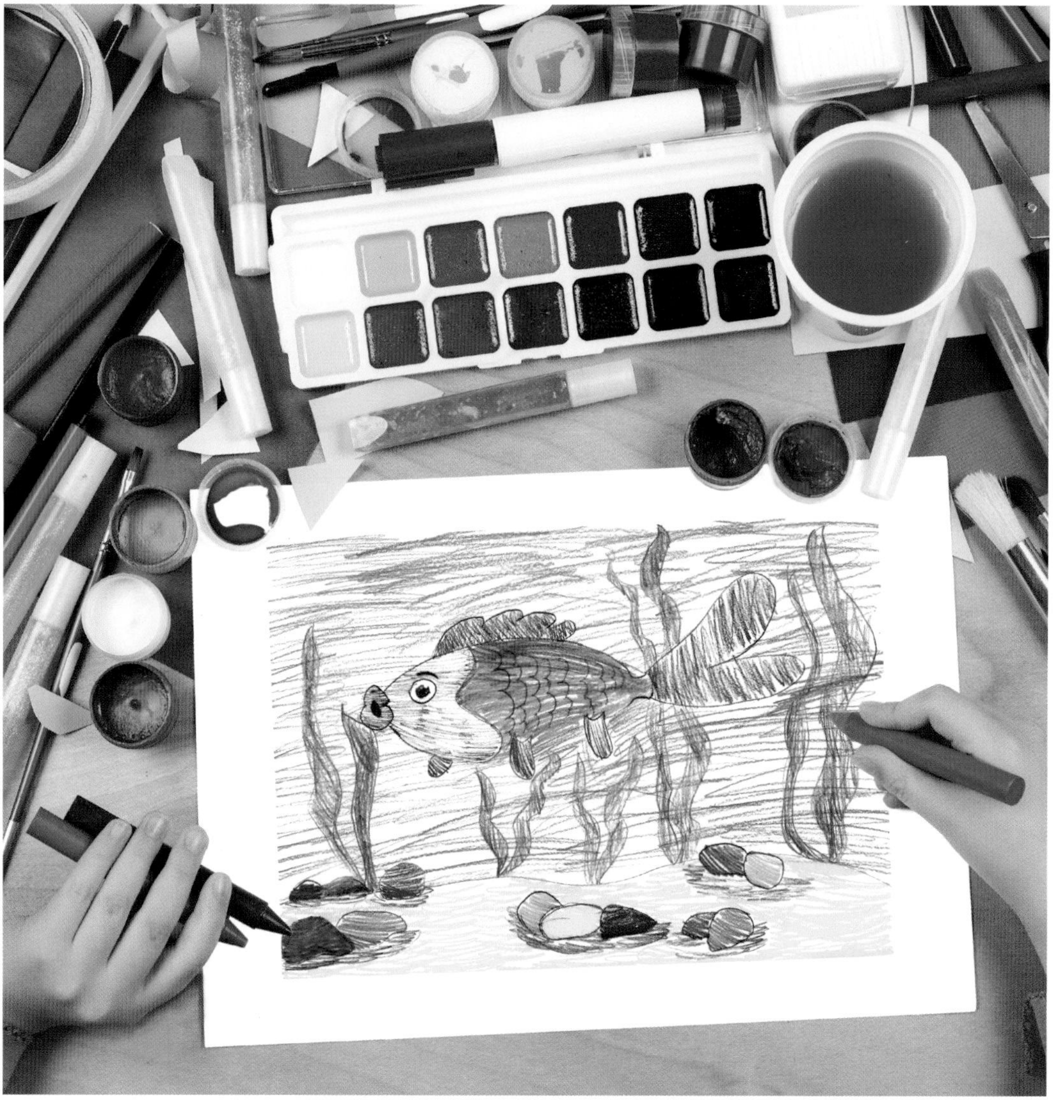

Answers on page 128.

Match It: page 6

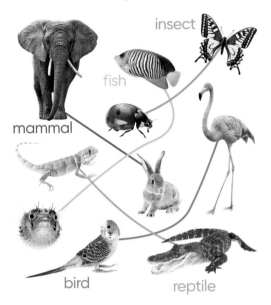

insect

fish

mammal

bird

reptile

What Do I Do?: page 8

A magnifying glass.
I make things look bigger to help people see them better.

What's Next?: page 7

Answers may vary.
One example: They go to the ocean.

Something's Wrong: page 9

Where Am I?: page 10

Flower

Fruit

Stems

Roots

On the Right Path: page 13

START

FINISH

Do It: page 11

The coconut cracked open.

What's Different?: page 14

Patterns: page 15

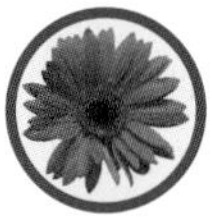

pink flower

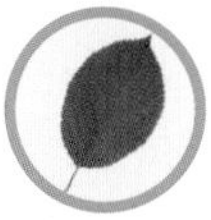

green leaf

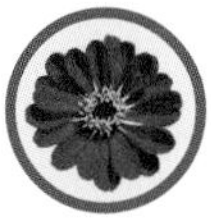

red flower

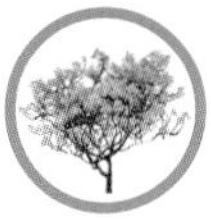

pink flowering tree

Memory: page 17

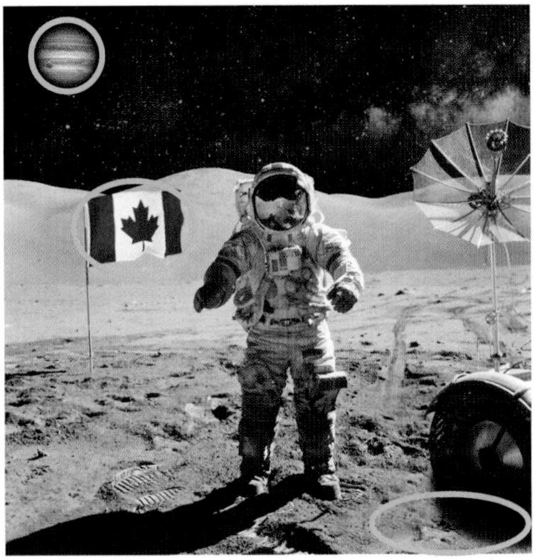

On the Right Path: page 16

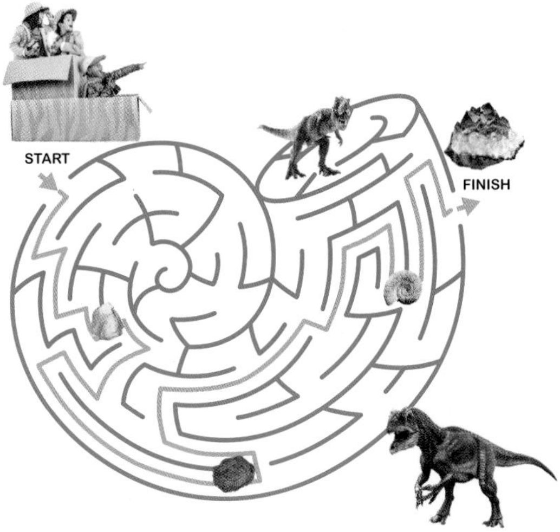
START
FINISH

What Do I Do?: page 19

A calculator.

I help people do math.

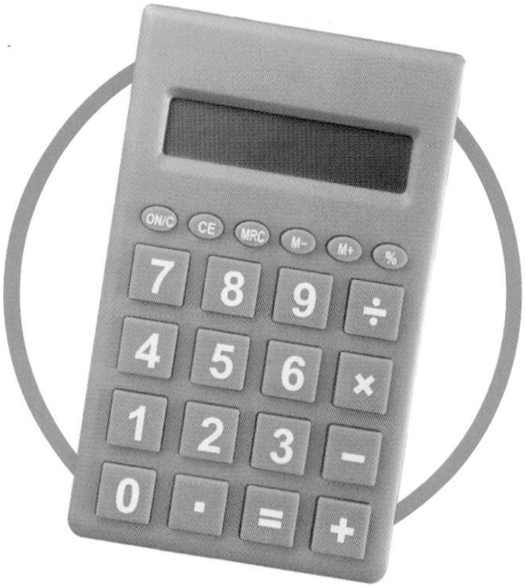

Answers

Corner of Your Eye: page 20

Answers vary. Generally, you will see movement first, then color, then shape.

Out of Order: page 23

Hide and Seek: page 22

Something's Wrong: page 24

110

Shadows: page 25

Draw It: page 27

Missing Piece: page 26

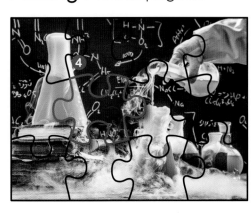

On the Right Path: page 28

Answers

Match It: page 29

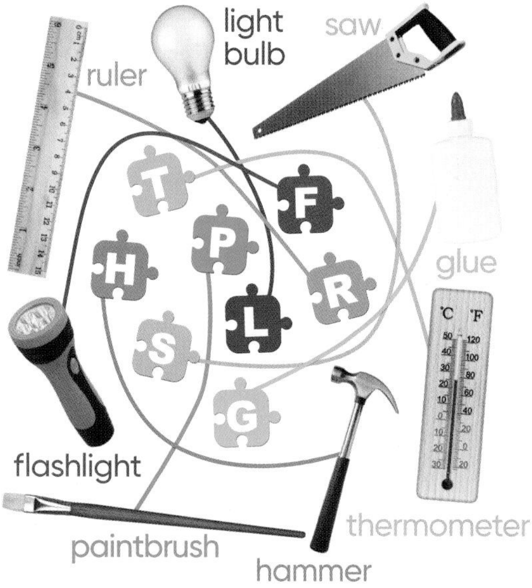
light
bulb
saw
ruler
glue
flashlight
thermometer
paintbrush
hammer

Zoom In: page 31

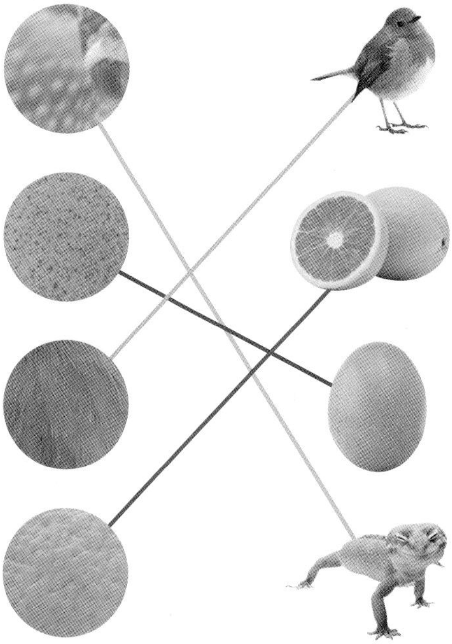

What Is It?: page 30

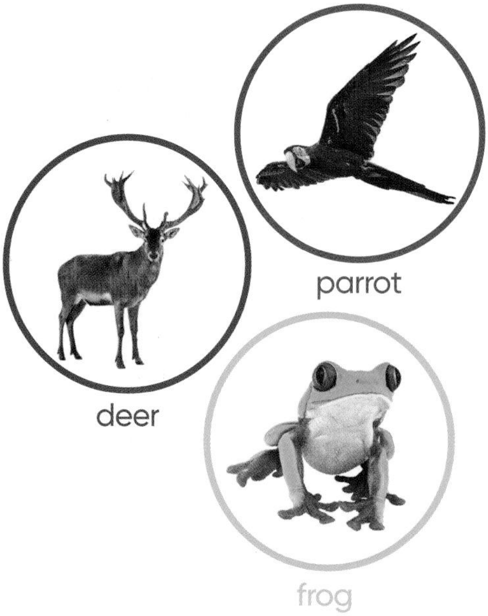
parrot
deer
frog

Where Am I?: page 32

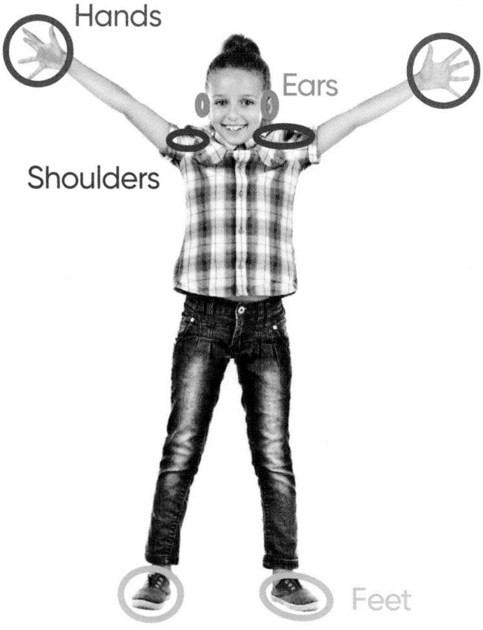
Hands
Ears
Shoulders
Feet

Which Ones?: page 33

Something's Wrong: page 35

Groups: page 34

Are yellow?
2 (lemon, sunflower)

Are flowers?
4 (chrysanthemum, gerbera, hydrangea, sunflower)

Can be eaten?
9 (cabbage, grapes, green beans, kiwi, lemon, okra, orange, strawberry, turnip)

Can grow in the garden?
13 (all of them)

Missing Piece: page 36

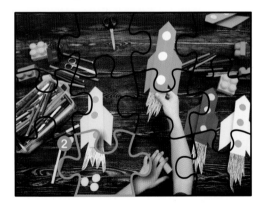

113

Answers

Clues: page 37

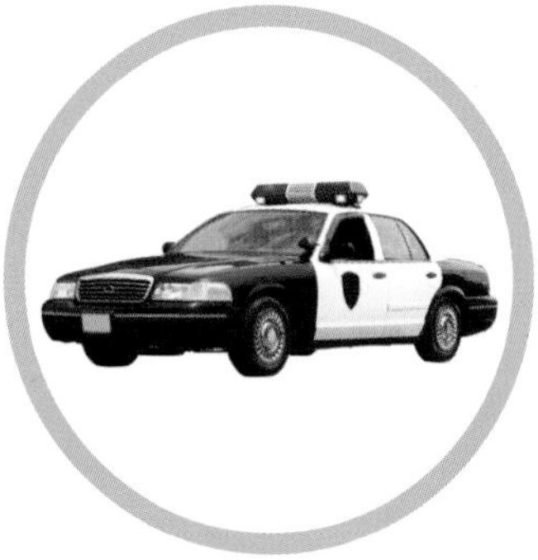

police car

On the Right Path: page 39

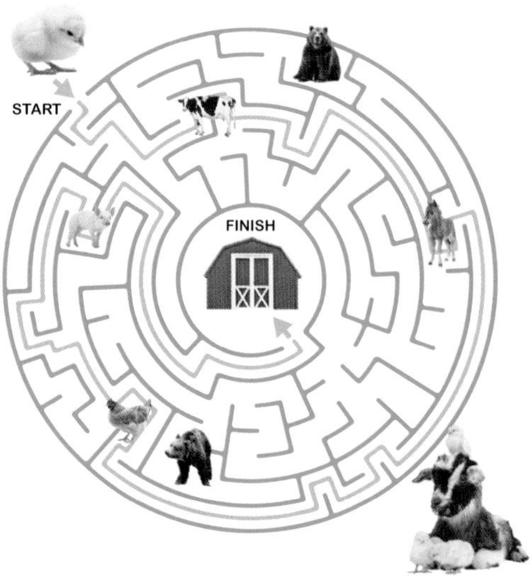

START
FINISH

What's Different?: page 38

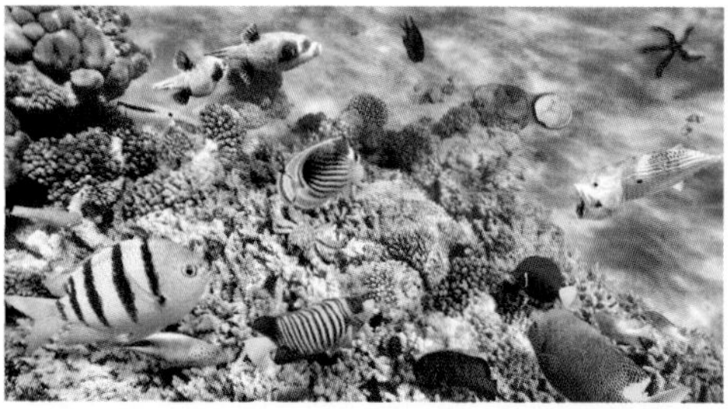

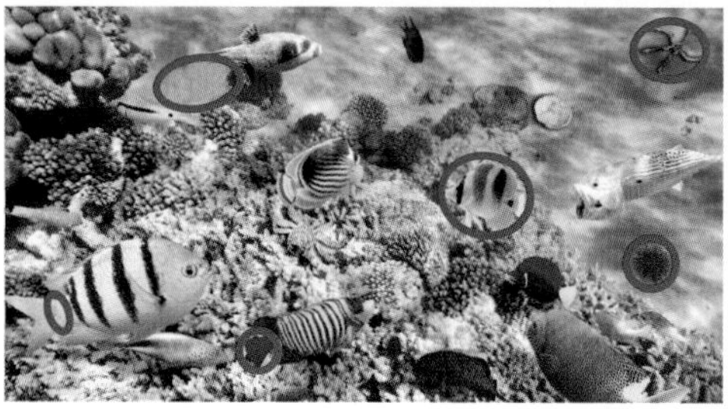

Hide and Seek: page 40

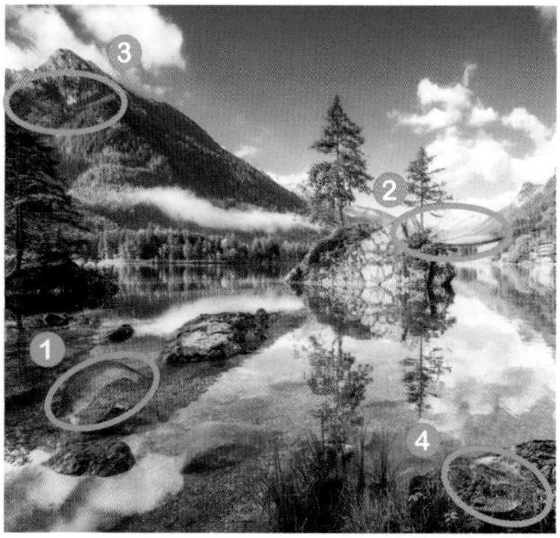

3
2
1
4

Memory: page 41

Zoom In: page 44

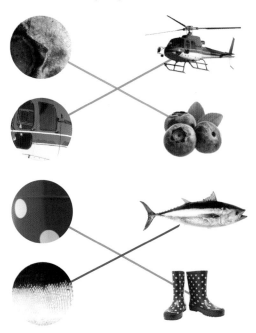

What's Next?: page 43

Answers may vary.

One example: The weather cools and becomes fall.

What's Different?: page 45

Taste Test: page 46

Answers vary.

What Do I Do?: page 49

A compass.

I help people draw circles.

Something's Wrong: page 48

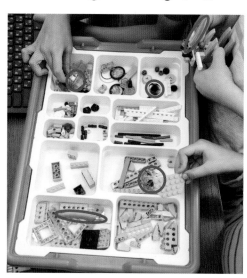

Out of Order: page 50

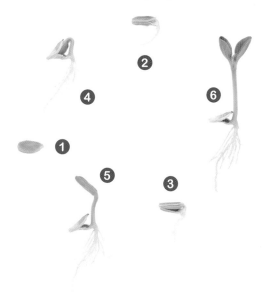

Match It: page 51

kangaroo
deer
fox
B
L
D
K
T
turkey
buffalo
P
F
G
goat
pigeon
lion

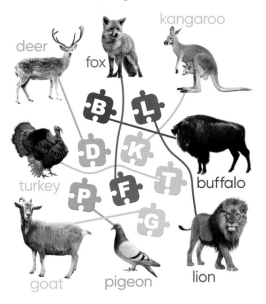

Do It: page 53

You blew bubbles.

Where Am I?: page 52

Wings
Eye
Beak
Talons
Tail

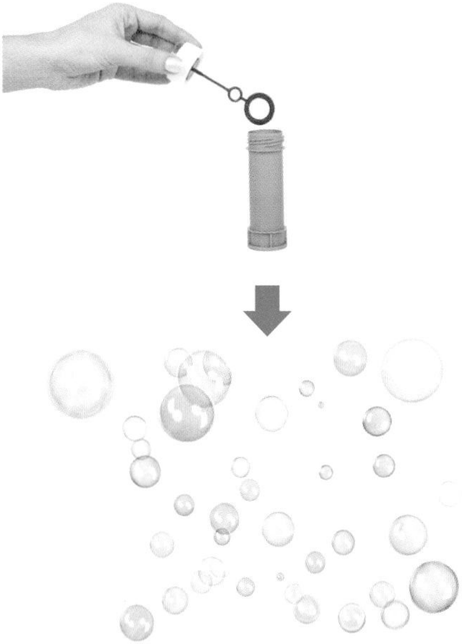

Shadows: page 55

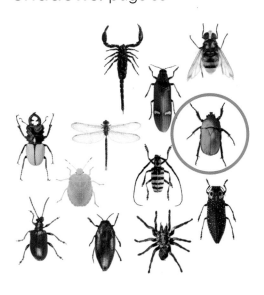

Missing Piece: page 56

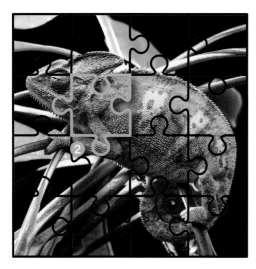

On the Right Path: page 58

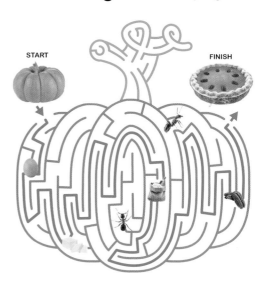

Draw It: page 57

Memory: page 59

Hide and Seek: page 61

Zoom In: page 63

What Is It?: page 62

microscope

bike

compass

Which Ones?: page 64

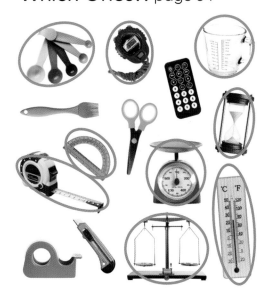

Answers

Shadows: page 65

Clues: page 67

clownfish

Groups: page 66

Are mammals?
6 (hedgehog, hippo, leopard, mouse, panda, raccoon)

Can fly?
4 (chicken, lovebird, owl, parakeet)

Are reptiles?
5 (crocodile, gecko, iguana, lizard, snake)

Have fur?
5 (hedgehog, leopard, mouse, panda, raccoon)

What's Next?: page 68

Answers may vary.
One example: A new moon, in a complete shadow.

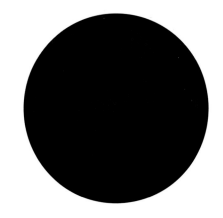

Draw It: page 69

Do It: page 71

The juice spilled.

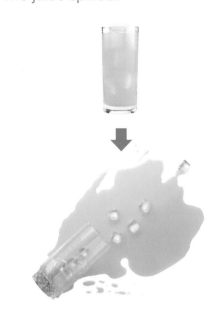

Patterns: page 70

 squirrel

 yellow butterfly

 grasshopper

 blue bird

On the Right Path: page 73

Match It: page 74

funnel
coat
beaker
tweezers
dropper
microscope
goggles
hourglass

Sink or Float: page 76

Answers may vary. Generally, packets should sink when you squeeze, rise when you let go.

Shadows: page 75

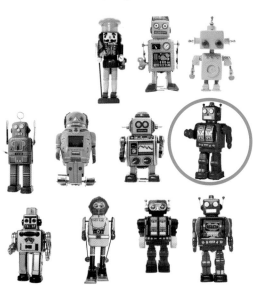

What Do I Do?: page 78

A telescope.

I help people see things in space.

What Is It?: page 79

salmon

octopus

hermit crab

Memory: page 81

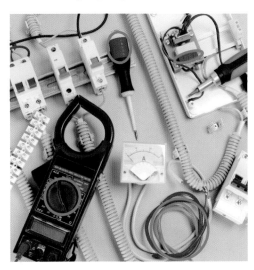

Where Am I?: page 80

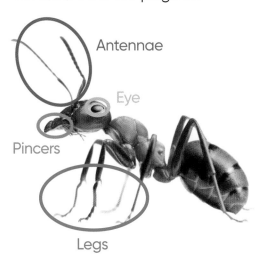

Antennae

Eye

Pincers

Legs

Out of Order: page 83

Answers

Missing Piece: page 84

Something's Wrong: page 86

Zoom In: page 85

Clues: page 87

ladybug

Groups: page 88

Are red?
2 (drill, scissors)

Are used to build?
6 (box cutter, drill, hammer, saw, scissors, stapler)

Help you see in the dark?
2 (flashlight, light bulb)

Have buttons?
2 (calculator, remote control)

What's Different?: page 90

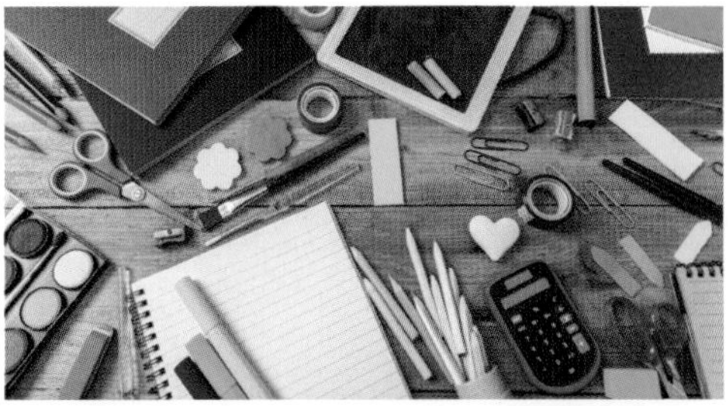

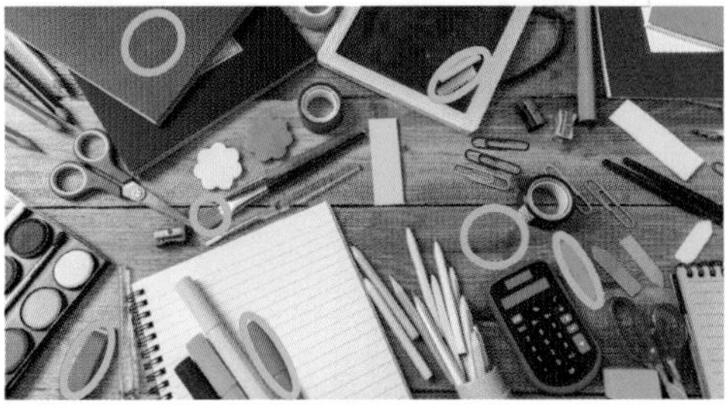

Which Ones?: page 89

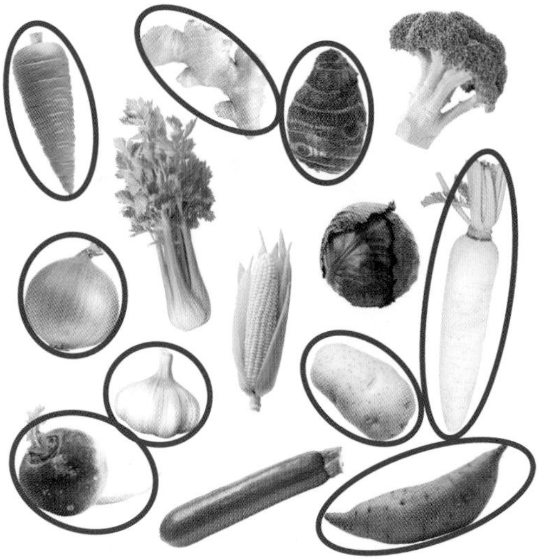

Patterns: page 91

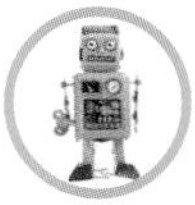 blue robot

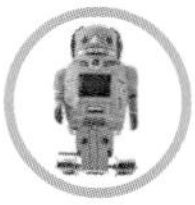 green robot

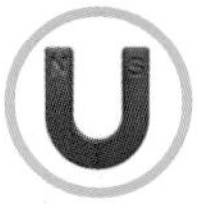 magnet

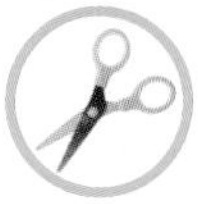 scissors

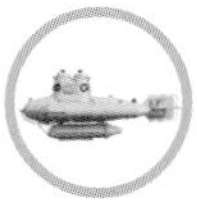 submarine

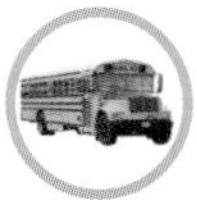 school bus

Hide and Seek: page 92

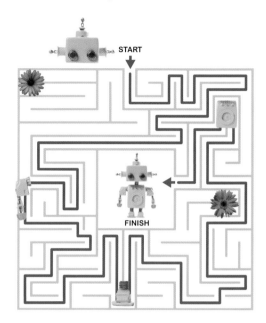

On the Right Path: page 94

Draw It: page 93

Patterns: page 95

 coral

 starfish

 clownfish

 angelfish

octopus

crab

Where Am I?: page 96

Answers vary.

Clues: page 99

compass

Shadows: page 98

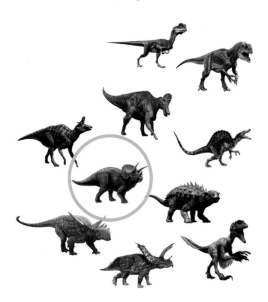

Where Am I?: page 100

From the left:

Sun ➔ Mercury ➔ Venus

➔ Earth ➔ Mars ➔ Jupiter

➔ Saturn ➔ Uranus ➔ Neptune

Out of Order: page 101

Do It: page 103

The balloon popped.

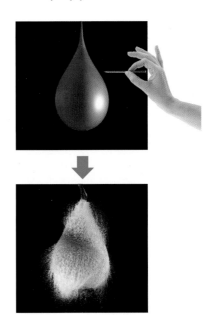

What Is It?: page 102

earth

spaceship

dinosaur

Memory: page 105